Governance

IN DARK TIMES

Governance

IN DARK TIMES

Practical Philosophy for Public Service

CAMILLA STIVERS

GEORGETOWN UNIVERSITY PRESS / WASHINGTON, D.C.

Georgetown University Press, Washington, D.C. www.press.georgetown.edu
© 2008 by Georgetown University Press. All rights reserved.

Library of Congress Cataloguing in Publication Data
Stivers, Camilla.
  Governance in dark times : practical philosophy for public service /
Camilla Stivers.
    p. cm.
Includes bibliographical references and index.
ISBN 978-1-58901-197-7 (alk. paper)
1. Public administration. 2. Public administration—Philosophy. I. Title.
JF1351.S845 2008
351.01—dc22

                    2007026038

⊚ This book is printed on acid-free paper meeting the requirements of the American National Standard for Permanence in Paper for Printed Library Materials.

15 14 13 12 11 10 09 08   9 8 7 6 5 4 3 2
First printing

Printed in the United States of America

What can I know?
What ought I to do?
What may I hope?

——IMMANUEL KANT

It is true of every conversation that through it something different has come to be.

——HANS-GEORG GADAMER

And since today the world has not yet blown away,
I take out fresh paper . . .

——TADEUSZ BOROWSKI

Contents

Acknowledgments

Like others who teach public administration classes filled with practicing administrators, since September 11, 2001, I have wrestled with the question of its lesson for professional public service education. This book is a product of that struggle.

I owe a great debt to the public administration students at the Maxine Goodman Levin College of Urban Affairs of Cleveland State University: undergrads, MPA students, and doctoral students. The vast majority are already professionals in public service, in government itself, or in community-based nonprofits. This book has benefited tremendously from their willingness to share insights on their lives in public service, and their unsparing but constructive critiques not only of specific chapters in earlier versions but also of my general approach to teaching ethics, administrative and organization theory, citizen participation, and management. Thank you, one and all.

Several colleagues read part or all of the manuscript in draft. I am grateful to Guy Adams, Larry Luton, Cynthia McSwain, and Orion White for making it better. Thanks to the anonymous reviewers, including five who commented on a description of the project *in embryo* several years ago. I am also particularly grateful to whoever it was who urged me to read Hobbes! Sharp questions from audiences at conferences and several universities also helped me to see many places where the arguments needed improvement.

My husband, Ralph Hummel, is in a class by himself. His commitment to philosophy in public administration has been an example to me, and he is an editor par excellence, wielding the editorial pen with the brio of Luke Skywalker and his light saber. He has saved me from a great deal of foolishness (not all of it scholarly), and our life together means more to me than I can say.

The book is dedicated to my grandchildren, Jeffrey Daniel, Matthew Jacob, and Leonora Camilla, who give me hope for brighter times.

Introduction

THE CATASTROPHIC EVENTS OF SEPTEMBER 11, 2001, BROUGHT Americans face to face with profound questions that in ordinary times people seldom consider. Few who watched the unfolding effects of the terrorist attacks, or read accounts of them, could have helped but feel the pity and terror that tragedy calls forth. The collapse of the World Trade Center towers, the destruction of a part of the Pentagon, and the actions of individuals who, faced with certain death, chose to spend their last moments preventing an airliner from finding its target—such spectacles seem at once to defy and to require understanding. Government efforts to strengthen homeland security and root out terrorists are no doubt important on a practical level. But they are overshadowed by images of direct confrontation with life and fate. The enormity of that day lingers, along with a sense of the fragility of our lives and those of the people we love.

Consider the words of two public servants who sifted through mounds of debris at the Fresh Kills landfill on Staten Island. They were looking to rescue and preserve objects as small as a quarter-inch in diameter. Their contact with the World Trade Center attack was more direct than most, but many Americans felt and thought as they did. "It's unnerving to realize that history happened," said FBI Special Agent Richard B. Marx as he selected items to go into museums. "It's made me more thankful for the things that can't be replaced in life. People, families, friendships. Things mean more to me than they used to. I cherish each moment I have now." They set about their unprecedented task with a sense of enormous responsibility: "We promised the families that we would look through everything," said police inspector James Luongo. They gradually evolved an ingenious sorting system as they worked. Surely there has never been so huge a culling of the precious from devastation, or one so filled with significance for the living.[1]

Many have pondered the sense of history that came to Special Agent Richard Marx in a hands-on way. The *New York Times* said that as a result of September 11, history had split into "before" and "after."[2] Others have suggested that we are in a "new world,"[3] a "new paradigm."[4] The United States may not be much more vulnerable to terrorist attack than it was on September 10, 2001, but its residents' *sense* of vulnerability is undoubtedly greater. Risk and danger are no longer "out there" but "over here."[5] And the danger is not only closer, it is also bigger and less predictable.[6] The cold war that once defined American perceptions of the place of the United States in the world order has been replaced by something called the War on Terror: A giant bull's eye has been replaced by a shooting gallery;[7] we're out of an iron cage and into a hall of mirrors.[8] As never before in our history, Americans feel themselves to be living in dark times.

Claims of darkness have been made about other historical moments. We call the European centuries following the fall of Rome "the dark ages." Certainly the twentieth century, with its two world wars, its atomic bombs, and its multiple genocides, seemed dark to many who lived through it. Philosopher Hannah Arendt, however, who fled for her life from the impending Holocaust, looked beyond the obvious dark times, "the disorder and the hunger, the massacres and the slaughterers" to another kind of darkness, one she saw lying at the root of visible events.[9]

The more fundamental darkness for Arendt comes from the disappearance of the public realm. This realm, said Arendt, ought to "throw light on the affairs of men by providing a space of appearances in which they can show in deed and word, for better or worse, who they are and what they can do."[10] Dark times, in the end, are not the consequence of monstrous events, which "are no rarity in history." They emerge from the loss of the political "world that lies between people," the space where different people come together to speak about shared concerns and hear what each believes to be the truth.[11] Such speech lights up a public world, where people are joined not in agreement but in commitment to struggle with important issues. Without this light, Arendt argued, people retreat into separate, private worlds, asking no more of politics than their rights and the freedom to pursue private interests. Deprived of the opportunity to hear and weigh the distinctive truths of others, people cling to "those 'best-known truths' which secretly scarcely anyone still believes in."[12] Meanwhile, the pillars of these truths have collapsed entirely (one can hardly avoid thinking of the World Trade Center towers). Humanity is standing in the midst of a veritable rubble heap—homeless in the most profound sense.

At this moment in history, the United States stands at the conjunction of two kinds of "dark times." First, there are the events: the attacks of September 11, 2001; the anthrax scares in Washington, D.C., later that fall; the aborted plan of the "shoe bomber"; the thwarted plot in 2006 to bring down several trans-Atlantic flights; the war in Iraq, to which there seems to be no acceptable end; and, it must be said, the horrific impact of hurricanes Katrina and Rita in August 2005—not terrorist attacks, to be sure, but no less a reminder of the fragility of life and the apparent inability of government to deliver on its promise to provide basic protection to U.S. residents.

Second, we have the dark times about which Arendt wrote: the loss of an active, vibrant public space in which ordinary citizens engage with the issues of the day. The question this book pursues is the connection between these two kinds of dark times. It explores the extent to which the loss of the public space renders us unable to come to grips with the existential impact of events that confront us with profound challenges to our sense of life's meaning. In particular, it will consider the meaning of public service in these doubly dark times.

To be sure, Hannah Arendt's vision of public space strikes many inhabitants of the early twenty-first century as romantic if not misguided. Few examples of such spaces come to mind, and many Americans are not sure they would want such spaces even if they were possible. The United States was founded on a vision of limited government, partly out of the desire to ensure individual liberty and partly out of the founders' skepticism about the qualifications of ordinary people for public decision making. The framers of the Constitution believed that by and large people were too self-interested and inexpert on public issues to be trusted with governing responsibility. Whether or not they were correct about the raw material the new nation started with, the system the founders set up had the effect of a self-fulfilling prophecy: By creating government with its centers of power remote and inaccessible to most citizens, they made sure that people would remain relatively uninvolved in governance, therefore ignorant about issues, unpredictable, and mistrustful of public authority.

Many public servants are equally skeptical. They do not see the desirability, let alone the possibility, of the kind of public space Arendt believed was the only real antidote to dark times. Faced with complex responsibilities, beholden to multiple masters (including agency heads, legislators, courts, interest groups, clients, and an amorphous but real "general public"), and pressed to meet numerical performance standards, public administrators tend to see an active citizenry as just one more factor that would further complicate already impossible jobs.

Nor do many see themselves as responsible for fostering public space. I once had a group of high-level federal managers—attendees at a Brookings Institution–sponsored workshop—tell me that citizen participation was fine in theory but had nothing to do with them. Many administrators would prefer not to consult or work with citizens, unless the law or program objectives make it necessary. Letting citizens in on things strikes administrators as risky ("We'll go over budget"; "They'll ask us for all kinds of things we can't do"). At the local level, some interaction with citizens is often built into the nature of the work; but at the state and federal levels, where the scope of responsibilities makes citizens remote from day to day activity, administrators tend to regard dialogue or collaboration with citizens as not part of their jobs, and the existence of public spaces as irrelevant, if not an out-and-out threat to administrative tranquility.[13]

The current gulf between government and citizens has many sources. They include scandals (beginning with Watergate), presidential candidates who promise to get government off the backs of the people, a tendency on the part of citizens to regard government as the enemy—even when they approve of the services they receive from it, and the very structure of American government, which offers limited possibilities for contact, let alone the exercise of authority by ordinary people. In recent years, prospects for bridging the gulf have dimmed with the rising tide of privatization and business thinking. Claims that the highest standard of public performance is running government like a business have weakened the sense that there is anything distinctive, much less uniquely valuable, about government. Public administrators are told that the most desirable way to fulfill their responsibilities is to farm them out to profit-making or nonprofit contractors. Whatever duties cannot be off-loaded are to be discharged in the most businesslike way possible. This trend (often called "devolution") has proceeded far enough that some scholars refer to contemporary government as "the hollow state."[14] In early 2007, the *New York Times* reported that contract volume had reached unprecedented levels, with amounts nearly doubling during the Bush administration.[15]

In the dark times since September 11, public servants—not to mention ordinary citizens—are in greater need than ever of finding meaning in public service, of grounding themselves in a sense of the public, of connecting and collaborating with other citizens. What they are being offered instead is an image of government as, at best, a business that doesn't make a profit and, at worst, an oppressive behemoth that threatens civil liberties. So pervasive is the reach of managerialism that the very word "governance" seems to have shifted its meaning.

Governance has long been used broadly to connote the exercise of various kinds of authority, as in "corporate governance," "nonprofit board governance," and so on. But in political and administrative theory, governance used to imply statecraft, that is, the exercise of distinctively governmental responsibilities. Statecraft used to be "the art of acting according to duty, justice, and reason on behalf of a community of citizens."[16] With the understanding of governance as management, however, more and more responsibilities have been contracted out or privatized entirely. The connotation of governance has expanded to include a panoply of nonprofit and business organizations while the image of the public "manager" has narrowed to dealmaker and contract monitor. The authority exercised directly by public officials has been reduced to little more than selecting contract recipients and ensuring that contract deliverables and other provisions are met. Once upon a time, administrators had to be prepared to show why contracting out was the best approach to serving the public interest. Now the burden of proof is reversed, and to not contract out they must demonstrate that the responsibilities in question are inherently governmental.

Fewer and fewer activities seem to meet this standard. Case in point: the $167.9 million local governance contract awarded in 2003 by the federal government to Research Triangle Institute, a nonprofit organization, to set up town councils and regional caucuses in Iraq. The contract was a *governance* contract: not for hauling away debris or restoring electrical systems, but for forming *governing* mechanisms in the region under occupation. Nevertheless, the project leader and his team saw it as another form of nuts and bolts: "There really is not a Sunni way to pick up garbage versus a Shiite way," he said, conflating service delivery with the development of democratic processes. Governance is delivering the goods. Meanwhile, neighborhood councils that blossomed spontaneously after the end of the first phase of the war were sidelined so that U.S. contractors could teach democracy to the Iraqis.[17]

My argument is that market understandings reflected in the new governance make each of us, inside and outside government, competitive individuals who connect out of self-interest and dissolve the connection when it no longer serves us. Dark times call for other connections than strictly instrumental ones. They call for the renewal of public spaces, for the creation of myriad opportunities for people—citizens, noncitizens, officials, and administrators—to meet so each can express his or her own viewpoint on the issues, great and small, that face us. I try to show how this vision, which I call governance of the common ground, is more plausible than it sometimes seems. My approach is to uncover philosophical assumptions supporting the mode of governance that has become so familiar, and to contrast them with an alternative set that I argue is equally plausible and has much to recommend it.

The destabilization caused by the events of September 11 evokes fear of further attacks that can happen anywhere, anytime. The giant storms of the last few years have ratcheted up the feeling of vulnerability. Each of us has a sense of crisis; we want to restore and maintain order—try to make existence revert to its former level of stability. The longing for order is understandable, but it is also hazardous. In the face of heightened risk, we are likely to accept measures imposed from above that promise greater safety but guarantee the reduction of freedom. Warrantless wiretapping and extended incarcerations without charges have been widely accepted by the public, perhaps because most people don't believe they will ever be the target of government surveillance.

There are other means of order, however, than tighter surveillance and stricter limits on movement and speech. Steps like these may turn out to be necessary on occasion, but they will not give us back the comfort we once took for granted. The events of September 11 have brought us to the edge of the abyss, face to face with the dread of untimely death. Our most important resource in this moment, I will argue, is one another, and the ties that connect us—not only family ties and friendships but also the public connections (Arendt called them the "in-betweens") that form when we meet and speak together, disagree and argue, about concerns we share.

To understand how to foster such connections and conversations, however, there is a need to think more deeply than we ordinarily do about basic elements in our current situation, particularly aspects highlighted by the events of the past decade. Arendt argued that in dark times the most important thing is not to rush to restore our former sense of safety, which she considered futile, but to *think*. By this she did not mean that we should strive to explain the causes of our predicament. Instead, we should simply try to understand events such as those of September 11, to acknowledge what happened, and "to endure this knowledge, and then to wait and see what comes of knowing and enduring."[18] In other words, as completely as Arendt believed that the root of dark times was the loss of public space, she would not have advocated specific remedies, at least until people had given themselves time to reflect and understand.

Arendt distinguished thinking from efforts to gather information and conduct scientific analysis. Not that such efforts were unimportant to her; she simply didn't believe that the results would give people in dark times what they most need: to put the public world together (that is, to make sense of it), not to take it apart. Thus, the immediate need to confront terrorism does not release us from the more fundamental necessity to "reconcile ourselves to reality, that is, try to be at home in the world."[19] Coming to terms with the existence of terrorism and the immediacy of its threat, or the inevitability of another devastating hurricane, does not imply resigning ourselves. It means accepting the fact that we live in a world where such things are possible and deciding what that implies. One point to consider is surely the extent to which terrorism should be taken as the factor that defines our entire situation. We can, if we choose, place terrorism in a broader framework of considerations, rather than simply letting its existence dwarf every other factor out of which we weave an understanding of our lives.

The discussion that unfolds in this book will have more to say about Arendt's ideas of understanding and thinking. For now, in a world we have been told is in the midst of unending war, it is enough to note that, as Arendt said, words used as weapons weaken understanding instead of promoting it: "Words used for the purpose of fighting lose their quality of speech; they become clichés. . . . The result of all such attempts is indoctrination," which destroys understanding.[20]

Political slogans have a way of turning off thinking instead of inspiring it. The first demand of the adherents of fundamentalist terrorism is commitment and obedience to commands, without question, without examination, without thought. If the fight against terrorism is to be more than a fight for sheer survival, we have to insist on moving past the superficial understandings offered us in speeches and press conferences, which aim to reduce the strangeness of a phenomenon like terrorism by linking it with one that is all too familiar: war. Understanding, if it comes at all, will come not by taking refuge in the familiar, but by "dissolv[ing] the 'known' into the unknown"—making life strange enough, through reflection, so that we see it with new eyes.[21]

In what follows, I dig below the surface of our current predicament in order to make certain aspects of it fresh enough to invite reflection. This is not a project that concludes by promulgating the "real meaning" of anything, including the war on terror, political life, or public service. My aim is to evoke thought and conversation. A public intellectual with whose ideas I disagree more often than not once said: "The most important task confronting Americans as a polity is, in part, a philosopher's task."[22] In my view, he is right. Bureaucrats and other public servants sometimes pride themselves on avoiding philosophy as impractical and affected. Yet at the same time most people in public life struggle to find the kind of meaning in it that brings human beings the sense that they are not wasting their lives. The approach of the book is premised on the usefulness of philosophy as a way to see things anew and deepen reflection. But if anything it has to say sheds light on dark times, it will only be because it stimulates readers to reflect on the meaning of their work in public service and start public-spirited conversations (arguments, more often than not) with the people around them. This hope is what lies beneath the discussions that follow, which take up questions such as what it means to think and judge.

Under the theme of light and darkness that weaves its way through the book are several issues. One is the darkness of terrorism and its relationship to enlightenment ideals upon which public life is grounded, such as rationality and progress. Heated rhetoric in the midst of the global war on terror overplays both the irrationality of the terrorist and the comforting solidity of reason. As much as the dynamics of public life revolve around rationality, a closer look suggests that it is not the solid, unarguable standard it sounds like. Enlightenment ideals still have force, especially Immanuel Kant's "Dare to know," but they must be reinterpreted for our times.

A central question about governance, particularly in the midst of a war on terror, has to do with security. Protecting people from one another and from outside attackers is the least debated role of government. Even advocates of extremely minimal states endorse it. The philosopher Thomas Hobbes argued that legitimate government was the product of mutual fear—that in the state of nature, people would agree with one another collectively to turn power over to the state in return for protection, and to renounce direct involvement in public life in favor of the liberty to pursue private interests. In recent years, this justification of government power is heard almost daily, in support of measures, such as secret surveillance and incarceration without specific charges, that would once have been regarded as illegitimate on their face. It is worth reflecting on the cost of this form of security and whether there is not another form worth reviving, grounded in ideas of mutual promising—

an American idea as old as the Mayflower Compact but comparatively neglected in public rhetoric.

The threat of terrorist attacks has reinvigorated another idea that can be traced to Hobbes: political realism. Being realistic and practical, or pragmatic, has always been a central guideline in public life, particularly in public administration—so taken for granted that questioning it can seem absurd. But realism has gained new life since September 11. As such it receives much attention in what follows out of the belief that leading a meaningful life in public service necessitates calling into question the very ideas and values we have so thoroughly internalized that we hardly know how to think otherwise.

What is entailed in saying that public servants govern? What political values does that statement support or undercut? Political questions like these ultimately have no correct answers, in the sense that empirical investigation does not give us proof of the assertions we make. Political questions can be—indeed must be—argued, but they cannot be settled once and for all. Political reflection, therefore, is argument that critically contests the views with which it disagrees, and that expects to be taken on by others. Much thinking in public administration (let alone public management) has been occupied with a search for right answers to administrative questions. Governance in dark times must first be consciously critical and philosophical for there to be an adequate foundation for finding plausible approaches to strategic and tactical questions (as Arendt would say, for public service to be about more than sheer survival).

Much of the following discussion focuses on the administrative aspects of governance rather than the legislative or judicial. Public service is a term broad enough to include judges, city council members, teachers, and those who work in nonprofit organizations. I have tried to make the argument fundamental to be of use to anyone in public life, including citizens. Often, though, my focus is on the work of the administrative agencies of government, not only because they are what I know best but more importantly because administration is the most permeable region of government, the one in closest proximity to citizens. Agencies are also the field upon which many of the issues that touch the lives of ordinary people are played out. Therefore they have the potential to stir direct interaction and dialogue—to create public worlds—that is being overlooked. This remains true even despite the "thinning out" of administration that has accompanied privatization and devolution.[23] Bureaucracy often takes the rap for government's remoteness and imperviousness, but in reality people interact directly with administrative agencies in a way they rarely do with legislators or the courts. (This assertion is becoming increasingly questionable at the hollowed-out federal level.) More often than not, these contacts are productive and successful: you get the driver's license you need without having to wait too long or fill out too many forms; the park ranger shows you where to find a pleasant campground or a hike with great views. Too often citizen contacts with public agencies are annoying or disheartening: you are refused the child care voucher you need to hire a babysitter so you can look for a job; the housing inspector reads you a list of rules instead of listening to your side of the story. For good or ill, though, administrative agencies do most of the work of government, the hands-on, direct activity that turns laws from mere words into events and accomplishments. Or at least they once did, before the tide of devolution swept through. This work has significance that goes far beyond achieving results or saving money—significance that may be worth fuller consideration than it often receives. In what follows I suggest that an important aspect of the significance of public service is its ability to connect with citizens.

This book was set in motion by the belief that many people in public life today, and especially those in the career civil service, have a clear perception of living in dark times but feel themselves alone in making sense of their experiences and finding meaning in their work. Gathering ideas from philosophy may offer new resources, especially if those ideas can be the basis for discussion.

I came to this belief not sitting by myself in my office but in the classroom in discussions with practicing administrators. During my twenty years as a teacher it has seemed to me that many practitioner-students come to graduate education hoping it will give them a toolkit. They often express the desire to learn the latest budgeting technique, or performance measurement strategy, or some other immediately practical instrument that will help them do their work more efficiently and effectively. This has always seemed completely understandable to me. Yet I generally resist this desire and try to gain their agreement for a different approach.

What classroom discussion gives practitioners they can get almost nowhere else is a chance to think, to step back from the stress and fast pace of daily responsibilities, and to reflect on bigger patterns and deeper questions than living the administrative life makes possible. My hope is this book will be the vehicle for reflection not only in classrooms but in other places where people in public life come together.

Part I considers what it means to think and to search for the truth in public life. The chapters in this part use philosophical perspectives to suggest how individual public servants might reflect on work and life in public service. Chapter 1 calls on two philosophers from different eras, Immanuel Kant and Michel Foucault, both of whom tried to answer the question "What is enlightenment?" As they struggled to answer this question they reflected on the nature of reason and what it means to be "enlightened." The argument of the chapter is that using your reason means thinking for yourself rather than depending on scientific, religious, or governmental authority. I suggest that this form of reason, which turns a critical eye on itself, sheds light in dark times. Chapter 2 explores truth in public service from the point of view of the question of torture. Although most public servants will never be called upon to torture anyone or even to facilitate torture, almost all of them have to come to grips with the nature of truth, particularly the kind based in scientific investigation (for example, the truths derived from policy analysis or from professional knowledge standards). Using selected philosophical perspectives on truth, the chapter shows how reflection on torture spotlights the tensions between knowledge and power that lurk inside government's dependence on "truth." Chapter 3 describes Hannah Arendt's understandings of thinking and judgment: how thinking, which Arendt called "the silent conversation between me and myself," sets up the possibility for exercising critical judgment and considered opinion. Arendt's arguments amount to an alternative model of reason, which I argue is another way of urging us to "dare to know."

Part II contrasts two models of public life, one based on Thomas Hobbes and one based on Arendt. In chapter 4 I describe these two models as divergent answers to the issue of security versus freedom in contemporary times, and ultimately to government's role in providing it. Hobbes's model, which sees the state as the top-down guarantor of safety from "the war of all against all," and the authority set up by contractual agreement among vulnerable humans out of mutual fear, is the one we take for granted. Arendt offers a different model, one based on the possibility of mutual promising and the light shed by public-spirited dialogue. Because this model seems unrealistic to many, chapter 5 explores philosophical assumptions of the two models: their contrasting views of social reality and human nature. I suggest that these views are not based on evidence; both are equally possible in theory. I argue that Arendt's view is actually more clear-sighted than Hobbes's and leads more plausibly in the direction of meaningful public life. Chapter 6 continues this line of thinking, presenting two views of governance: the Hobbesian one that supports current managerial understandings of governance, and one based in Arendt and in Mary Parker Follett, which I call governance of the common ground.

In part III, I offer two concluding reflections on public service. Chapter 7 explores pragmatism as a framework for action in public service. The discussion draws out the difference between the familiar connotation of pragmatism as nuts-and-bolts realism and the richer ideas in pragmatist philosophy. I use John Dewey's understanding of democracy as a form of associated living to suggest democratic approaches to administrative decision making—approaches that are practical in a deeper sense. Chapter 8 offers a developmental public service ethic. I argue that beneath professional codes and agency rules, beneath the situational challenges that mark bureaucratic decisions, is each public servant's sense of self, and a surrounding matrix of relationships that either support or undercut leading an ethical life. This vision is at the heart of the book's argument.

In sum, dark times are darker than we know. They make us want to cling together and stamp out disagreement (as when "patriotism" requires refraining from criticism). Worse, dark times drive us apart, so that each of us retreats into a private world and bars the door against politics. The darkness of the threat of terrorism is immediate, but equally profound is the darkness of a lost public world. As the men at Fresh

Kills said, as they sifted through the wreckage of the Twin Towers in search of small bits of stuff that would mean something to survivors (that is, to all of us), catastrophes remind us of what's really important. I would add, they summon us to think.

NOTES

1. Glenn Collins, "One Recovery Effort Is Over; One Is But Begun," *New York Times*, November 25, 2003, A23.

2. Quoted in Donald Kettl, *System under Stress: Homeland Security and American Politics* (Washington, DC: CQ Press, 2004), 3.

3. James Bamford, *A Pretext for War: 9/11, Iraq, and the Abuse of American Intelligence* (New York: Doubleday, 2004), 104.

4. Daniel Benjamin and Steven Simon, *The Age of Sacred Terror: Radical Islam's War against America* (New York: Random House, 2002), 222.

5. Greg Bankoff, "Regions of Risk: Western Discourses on Terrorism and the Significance of Islam," *Studies in Conflict and Terrorism* 26 (2003).

6. Philip Heymann, *Terrorism, Freedom, and Security: Winning without War* (Cambridge, MA: MIT Press, 2003).

7. Bamford, *Pretext for War*, 213.

8. Mikkel Vedby Rasmussen, "A Parallel Globalization of Terror: 9/11, Security and Globalization," *Cooperation and Conflict: Journal of the Nordic International Studies Association* 37 (2002): 328.

9. Hannah Arendt, *Men in Dark Times* (San Diego: Harcourt Brace, 1968), viii.

10. Ibid.

11. Ibid., 11.

12. Ibid., 10.

13. These comments are based mainly on my conversations over the last twenty years with public administrators in classes at Cleveland State University and The Evergreen State College, as well as in career executive training sessions sponsored by the State of Washington, Cleveland State University, and the Brookings Institution.

14. See H. Brinton Milward, Keith Provan, and Barbara Else, "What Does the Hollow State Look Like?" in *Public Management Theory: The State of the Art*, ed. Barry Bozeman (San Francisco: Jossey-Bass, 1993).

15. Scott Shane and Ron Nixon, "In Washington, Contractors Take On Biggest Role Ever," *New York Times*, February 4, 2007, 1.

16. James G. March and Johan P. Olsen, *Democratic Governance* (New York: Free Press, 1995), 5.

17. Naomi Klein, "Hold Bush to His Lie," *The Nation*, February 23, 2004, 10.

18. Hannah Arendt, "Understanding and Politics," *Partisan Review* 20 (1953): 378.

19. Ibid., 377.

20. Ibid., 378.

21. Ibid., 382.

22. George Will, *Statecraft as Soulcraft: What Government Does* (New York: Touchstone/Simon and Schuster, 1983), 11.

23. See Larry D. Terry, "The Thinning of Administrative Institutions," in *Revisiting Waldo's Administrative State: Constancy and Change in Public Administration*, ed. David H. Rosenbloom and Howard E. McCurdy (Washington, D.C.: Georgetown University Press, 2006), 109–28.

PART I

Thinking, Reason, and Truth
PHILOSOPHY FOR PUBLIC SERVICE

CHAPTER I

Rethinking Reason after September 11

FOR A TIME IT SEEMED THAT THE ATTACKS ON SEPTEMBER 11, 2001, marked a watershed in American public consciousness. For many decades Americans had comforted themselves with the idea that terrible things happen, but they generally happen elsewhere. We told ourselves that we fight wars, but we don't fight them within our own borders. Famines and epidemics happen in what we call the third world. We export medicine, food, and development overseas, but the risk of disaster stays there. The terrorist attacks on September 11 wrenched Americans out of a long-standing complacency. In that sense the attacks challenged a proposition we tend to take for granted: that America is somehow different, meaning better.

In the aftermath Americans were encouraged to see the nation in the grip of a perpetual state of crisis. Stepped-up security measures in airports and at border crossings were constant reminders of insecurity; however, they quickly became more annoying or stressful than reassuring. Frequent alerts about changes in the official threat level (yellow, orange) seemed to tell people how afraid to be without identifying what the specific threat was or where and when it might strike. The war in Iraq only exacerbated the sense of crisis. Yet a disconnect persisted. Government tried to make people feel safe, but many Americans continue to believe that little can be done to prevent further attacks.

Consider, for example, the comments of a few ordinary citizens after the threat level was raised from yellow to orange in August, 2004. Some were cynical: "I don't believe anything they tell us," said Kenosha, Wisconsin, diner-owner John Gilmore, "there's always an ulterior motive somewhere." Cleveland hot dog stand operator Bryan Kupetz declared, "I wouldn't be surprised if they caught Osama bin Laden two days before the election." Others struggled to hang on to a modicum of trust in government. Lawyer Ron Greenspan said, "The thought of a president using this for political gain is just disgusting. I have a hard time believing that a man of his political stature would do that." In New York, broker assistant Keith Kirlew commented, "You have to hope it's true. If this is political, it's pretty sick, so I have to assume there's some truth to it."[1]

Several years after the September 11 attacks, few people continue to see reality as completely transformed. Nevertheless, few see their lives or their picture of the world as unchanged. The planners of the attacks hoped to instill permanent fear. Terrorism is meant to terrify. Their intent was less strategic than symbolic—hence the choice of targets. The terrorists staged a horrific piece of theater, a spectacle meant to convey to Americans that their days of complacent comfort and feeling of invulnerability were over. We were forced to come face to face with a world that had *already* changed. In that world the might of the United States was not as unqualified as most Americans had once assumed.[2]

In this regard the terrorists scored a big victory. A source—perhaps *the* source—of the power of terrorism is that the more we talk about it, the more visibility it has and the more it subtly pervades and reshapes ordinary life.[3] This line of thought suggests that by declaring war on terrorism, the Bush administration gave the terrorists exactly what they wanted. Osama bin Laden and his followers see their struggle in the same way as America's leaders: as a war.[4] Seeing the struggle as a war encourages images that sharpen the contrast between the two sides: us vs. them, the forces of darkness vs. the forces of light, the civilized vs. the barbarian, evildoers vs. good guys. These images have become so pervasive in American public life since the attacks that now it is the images, rather than our former comfort, that are in danger of being taken for granted. Seeing themselves as on the side of good, of light, of civilization makes people feel safer and blameless. It's those others who are barbarians, evildoers, sons of darkness. By insulating ourselves in this way, we increase the likelihood that when future attacks occur we will react without thinking.

At the same time it seems to be difficult for most people to stay at a high level of alertness to potential threat. Philosophers who reflect on the quality of human experience have called ordinary daily life the "daylight" side of existence. In contrast, crises such as September 11 "constitute a 'night side' . . . a constant threat to the taken-for-granted, matter-of-fact, 'sane' reality of life in society." Such events bring us face to face with the deaths of others and, therefore, with the prospect of our own death, which is "the most terrifying threat. . . . The integration of death within the paramount reality of social existence is, therefore, of the greatest importance for any institutional order." Human beings cannot stay in immediate touch with the ultimate terror of death. Once a threat to ordinary life has receded from immediacy, or in order to ensure that it *does* recede, human beings contain it by pushing it behind a sense of normality.[5]

The darkness that terrorism has thrust us into must be explored. At one level, darkness is obvious. The terrorists meant to terrify and they succeeded, if only for a time. On reflection, however, the situation in which we find ourselves can open other avenues of meaning. A place to start is the possibility that terrorism may *not* be a radical alteration of our world. Instead it may be a particularly powerful indicator of fundamental aspects of the modern age.

THE MODERN

What is it to be modern? Most people think first of technological advancement. Modernity gives up magical or supernatural ways of knowing in favor of rationality. Max Weber, theorist of modern bureaucracy, said "The fate of our times is characterized by rationalization and intellectualization and, above all, by the 'disenchantment of the world.'" Weber saw "rational, empirical knowledge" as the source of the disenchantment, which he believed transformed the world from a realm of magic and mysticism "into a causal mechanism."[6]

Societies are modern not only because of a reliance on science and technology but because they look to impersonal rules and standard procedures (laws and regulations) as the basis for legitimate authority rather than to the personal qualities of a charismatic individual or to cultural or religious traditions. Modern rationalism entails clearly defined concepts and means-ends calculations, systematic rather than arbitrary modes of thought, pursuing fixed goals as directly and efficiently as possible, and specifying and following formal methods to reach knowledge. Weber regarded bureaucracy as the embodiment of modern rationality; little wonder, then, that public servants find these characteristics familiar.

But rationality contains certain forces that keep it from operating perfectly and completely.[7] The title of a frequently cited book, *All That Is Solid Melts into Air: The Experience of Modernity*, illustrates this ambivalence. The first part of the title is a quote from Karl Marx, well known for his view of society as a totally objective ("solid") realm driven toward its destiny by economic conditions. Clearly Marx saw social reality as solid. What was melting were the illusions people had accumulated. Marx observed "All that is solid melts into air, all that is holy is profaned, and men at last are forced to face with sober senses the real conditions of their lives and their relations with their fellow men."[8] The coming to terms with reality Marx forecasted mirrors Weber's disenchantment. Both men understood modernity as the stripping away of misapprehensions about the workings of society. The vertigo Marx described as characteristic of the modern is still perceptible today, especially when something disrupts the settled views on which we ordinarily base our reactions to events.

Anthony Giddens argues that modernity is characterized by radical doubt that can be traced to the philosopher Descartes, who came to his famous "I think, therefore I am" dictum only after doubting the reality of everything. In the modern age, Giddens says, all knowledge consists of hypotheses, or "claims which may very well be true, but which are in principle always open to revision and may have at some point to be abandoned."[9] Most of the time such tentative knowledge serves human beings *relatively* well (perhaps the pun is warranted). But it offers a rather tenuous kind of security or trust in the world's continuance in the form we are used to. Even equipped with practical consciousness, the taken-for-granted rules and understandings people share with others about how to go on in daily life, the modern individual is never far from the chaos that threatens when shared reality is breached.[10] Taken-for-granted daily life screens out the shakiness of our faith in objective reality and helps keep us from feeling the radical doubt that caused Descartes to recoil—the genie that has never quite been put back into the philosophical bottle. Not too far beneath the fabric of daily life is dread, or "the prospect of being overwhelmed by anxieties that reach to the very roots of our coherent sense of 'being in the world.'" Giddens argues that in a globalized world people feel a sense of big risks from which no one is completely out of reach and, at the same time, a sense of being in the cocoon of daily life, trusting in the continuation of its routines. Daily life is uneventful. But the possibility of fateful moments is always there—and since September 11, Americans know it unmistakably.[11]

Globalization only strengthens the feeling of being swept up in forces no one individual, group, or government can fully control—even the powerful United States. In a global world there is no longer any "outside" to which to banish threats: no way to draw firm boundaries, no shelter, no means of escape. The fall of the Berlin wall ended an era that began with the Great Wall of China and Hadrian's Wall in Britain—fortifications built to keep out barbarians and other threats. But as barriers erected in Israel and along the southern U.S. border show, no wall is thick enough or high enough today.[12]

Yet the daily news is filled with vain efforts to strengthen boundaries:

- The federal government opens new airbases on the Canadian border so planes can look for smugglers and others crossing illegally.[13]
- A married couple, one Dane, one New Zealander, are denied permission to live in Denmark. The Danish government explains its policy as "an unavoidable result of the effort to reduce the influx of foreigners, who . . . burden the social welfare system, commit more than their share of the crime and tend to form enclaves within Denmark, defying efforts to integrate them."[14]
- In Bolivia, Santa Cruz province is thinking about seceding. Its residents are sure that the region's resources and economic drive are unfairly subsidizing the rest of the country. One leader of the secession movement refers to the region as "a nation without a state."[15]

- In the throes of violent unrest on the part of French citizens who feel rejected by French society, one man exclaims: "I was born in Senegal when it was part of France. I speak French, my wife is French and I was educated in France." The problem is "the French don't think I'm French."[16]

Modernity, then, is a mixed phenomenon: It is defined by sophisticated technology and rationality but in practice unable to deliver fully on its promise of speeding up and smoothing out society's drive toward its goals and unable to close itself off completely from the influence of unpredictable forces and events. Despite the efforts of experts and leaders to strengthen security measures, despite the routines of daily life, fateful moments occur. The boundaries—physical and mental—erected to hold chaos at bay cannot be sustained in the face of such moments.

Modernity will always run up against the impossibility of achieving complete predictability. From time to time, forces that resist rationalization will show themselves in one way or another. The terrorism of al-Qaeda or the insurgents in Iraq reflects this paradox. (So do catastrophes like hurricanes and tsunamis.) From one angle, fundamentalist terrorism seems nonmodern, even antimodern. Islamist terrorists are guided by traditional sources of authority and charismatic leaders like Osama bin Laden. However, this form of terrorism depends on modern technological tools such as the Internet, the jumbo jet, and high-tech weapons. On reflection, Islamist terrorism appears complex enough that the dichotomies of civilized versus barbaric, modern versus primitive don't fit very neatly.

As September 11 shows, it is possible that modernity provides no sure protection from forces it harbors and conceals. In the face of such events, people are subject to being swayed by images of us versus them that imply that future fateful moments can be predicted and forestalled. They will buy the idea that if they just accept a tough enough Patriot Act, America can keep out the forces of darkness. Images of evildoers lure the country toward the notion that terrorists are so different that they cannot be understood, only eliminated.

The word "understood" seems to imply excusing someone for a terrible deed. Yet understanding does not necessarily imply forgiveness, according to Hannah Arendt. The two are quite different. Forgiveness is a single act, one that wipes the slate clean. Understanding, on the other hand, is unending, because it is a lifelong effort to reconcile ourselves to the world.[17] It takes conscious effort to come to terms with an existence in which events such as those of September 11 happen. It takes reflection to resist attempts by spinmeisters and the powerful people they serve to shape the meaning of events and actions by packaging them to serve their own ideologies. When told that we are in the midst of a global war on terror, it is easy to jump to the conclusion that, like other wars, it can be won—the evil can be eliminated. And if *this* evil, why not *all* evil? Just continue to vote for the good guys!

On the other hand, if terrorism can be seen as a roundly denied *part* of modernity (rather than its opposite), which shows itself despite all efforts to keep it at bay, this might be the starting place for coming to terms, as Arendt advised, with something basic about human existence. At the very least it might induce a healthy skepticism about proposals that promise, in return for political support, to restore illusory security. Acceptance that there is no way to "annul or neutralize the eventfulness of the event," in order to immunize ourselves against another one in the future, "is not to go against reason" but is "in fact the only chance to think, rationally, something like a future and a becoming of reason"—that is, to expand our understanding of what reason is.[18] The potential for that future and that becoming occupies the rest of this chapter.

THE ENLIGHTENMENT

Western belief in the power of reason is a product of the Enlightenment, an intellectual movement in eighteenth-century Europe marked by "a general commitment to . . . emancipating mankind, through knowledge, education and science, from the chains of ignorance and error, superstition, theological dogma, and the dead hand of the clergy; to instilling a new mood of hope for a better future . . . ; and to practical action for creating greater prosperity, fairer laws, milder government, religious tolerance, intellectual freedom, expert administration, and not least, heightened individual self-awareness."[19] This summary captures the importance that Enlightenment thinkers placed on the use of reason and their optimism that reason would bring both better living conditions and greater political freedom. Reason as expressed and fulfilled in the accumulation of knowledge—especially the results of scientific investigation—would make effective practical activity possible and almost literally bring light where darkness had been. Human beings would not only see the truth, they would see it for themselves rather than have it handed to them by religious leaders and other authorities.

The importance that Enlightenment thinkers placed on changing the role of religion in society can be traced to religious wars that had wracked Europe with violence for generations. Their idea was not to get rid of religion entirely; instead, it was to put boundaries around it and shift it from the political center of society to an honored but limited position. The source of the state's legitimacy moved from God ("the divine right of kings") to the people and the idea of a contract between ruler and ruled. The people gave up a limited amount of freedom in return for order. The state was no longer embodied in the monarch (as in Louis XIV's famous *"L'état, c'est moi"*) but in the nation—the great body of the people. In this sense, the whole point of the Enlightenment was to replace reverence for God-given authority, at least in public affairs, with rules arrived at through the imaginative use of reason.[20] The modern state makes room for religion and ensures its free practice but is itself secular. This aspect of modernity presents the greatest contrast with religious fundamentalism, with its belief that religion should permeate all aspects of existence and that religious authority should be preeminent in governing.

Enlightenment thinkers taught that light means truth, knowledge, and the use of reason; darkness, by implication, means error, ignorance, and the unquestioning acceptance of authorized versions of the truth, rather than finding it for oneself. But interestingly the Islamist terrorists use the same Manichaean light-dark images to describe Americans as our leaders use about them. Both President George W. Bush and Osama bin Laden see the struggle as one between the Sons of Light and the Sons of Darkness, in which everyone must choose up sides and there is no such thing as neutrality or compromise.[21]

Longing for the lost sense of safety, together with pressure to demonstrate unquestioned patriotism, increases vulnerability to imagery and stereotyping. Us/them perceptions are reinforced: not only terrorists versus civilization, the godly versus the ungodly, but also Republicans versus Democrats, "girlie-men" versus tough guys, and so on. The more such imagery permeates public debate, the weaker the notion of reasoned argument seems.

The very idea of public service is rooted in the use of reason rather than unthinking adherence to orders from on high. Service has never implied slavish obedience. Most administrative work requires interpretation of orders, whether they come from a supervisor or directly from the law itself. Public service depends on the use of judgment about which aspects of relevant laws pertain in particular cases and why. Public administrators are expected to answer for their decisions, to make a reasoned case for what they do. The persistence of public-interested reasoning as a norm for public life is attested to by the sense of outrage we feel when it is ignored—for example, when a health data analyst is prevented by his boss from sharing cost projections with Congress because they undermine the administration's case for the Medicare drug bill, or when the Defense Department official in charge of procurement awards a huge contract to the corporation that has offered her a job and tolerated her low-performing daughter.[22]

In the contemporary public conversation, however, us/them imagery threatens to transform reasoned argument, if not replace it, so that the difference between reasons and stereotypes disappears. If the explanation given for locking someone up without a charge and without access to counsel is "we have to protect ourselves from *them*," the very nature of reason is called into question—though it goes unnoticed. Simply put, not just any old explanation will do. The bases of reasoned argument are meant to make us reflect, not react without thinking.[23] All this suggests that it may be worth taking a closer look at enlightenment. What can be made today of the eighteenth-century belief in reason and its potential to free humankind from mental and political bonds? Dark times call us to reassess our taken-for-granted notions of rationality and its importance in public life: not to give up on reason, but to see it in a new way.

Two Thinkers on Enlightenment: Kant and Foucault

A frequently cited example of Enlightenment thinking is Immanuel Kant's essay, "An Answer to the Question: What Is Enlightenment?" The essay first appeared in the *Berlinische Monatsschrift* in December, 1784. Kant defines enlightenment as the capacity "to use one's intelligence without the guidance of another." We show our intellectual immaturity when we rely on a book to tell us what some event means, on a pastor to tell us what is right and wrong, on a doctor to tell us how to eat. Kant's message: "*Sapere Aude!* [Dare to know!] Have the courage to use your own intelligence!"[24]

For a philosopher living in the Prussia of Frederick the Great, this might seem a daring message. And in fact Kant qualified his advice. Reversing the ordinary meanings of the words "private" and "public," he argued that in what today we call public service, in a "civic post," reason is *private*. In the performance of the duties of office, it is proper that laws and customs rein in the free use of the individual's reasoning powers. *Public* reason, on the other hand, meant speaking freely as a "private" citizen about public matters. Kant justified limits on an individual's exercise of reason on the job because he or she is answerable to authority. But when the individual citizen speaks to the public world, the exercise of reason must be completely unfettered, even (or especially) when what he or she says is critical of politics, religion, or widely held intellectual beliefs.[25]

This position was riskier than it seems today. We are used to free speech; Kant was not. His sovereign, Frederick the Great, responded to his call for public reason this way, "Dispute as much as you want and about what you want, but obey!" And in fact, nine years after the essay appeared, Kant was chastised by the official censor for comments in his *Religion within the Limits of Reason Alone* and forced to apologize.

The whole of Kant's philosophy was grounded in the idea that "to criticism everything must submit." *Everything* included even reason itself. Reason has to examine not only public debate and religious orthodoxy but also the foundations of its own operations. Reason must shine its light on its own workings, but it can never fully establish its own grounds. You can't reason your way to a complete justification of reason. At some point you simply have to declare your commitment to it.

Therefore reason contains an element of paradox: its operations are absolutely legitimate but also impossible to self-legitimize completely.

There is an unresolved tension in Kant's argument. On one hand, he insisted that specific historical conditions had to be taken into account in assessing a particular use of reason. On the other, he claimed to have identified aspects of human intellect—understanding, reason, judgment—that transcended all context. What partly resolves this tension is that the mind is free rather than bound by necessity. Human nature, as nature, can't be fully understood and brought under scientific laws in the same way as chemistry or geology. On the contrary, the human mind has the capacity to develop its use of reason (*Sapere Aude!*). In this lies its freedom. The possibility exists for humankind to grow in wisdom.[26]

This tension in Kant between his desire for a concept of universal reason and his commitment to human freedom suggests how paradoxical modernity is. Using science and technology, we moderns want to bend nature to our will, but it is human freedom that unavoidably escapes our control. History, or human action, cannot be brought under causal laws in the same way chemical reactions can. We can give an account of a human event and interpret its meaning, but we can't explain it in the same definitive way as the interaction between two physical substances. One of the reasons fateful moments like September 11 hit technologically advanced societies so hard is that people tend to block from their minds both the possibility of such events and their source—freedom.

Kant's definition of enlightenment implies the potential for growth in wisdom, by individuals and by society. The most important thing about this potential is that its direction and shape are fundamentally unpredictable. This is because growth depends on the free exercise of reason: not completely pure reason unaffected by the conditions around it but still free in the sense that conditions are not sufficient to determine its content. This means that societies can set up agendas for progress, but the process will inevitably be transformed by the operations of human minds and wills (as well as, of course, by fateful moments like September 11).[27] Kant's vision of human action as belonging to nature yet outside the realm of cause and effect has been challenged often, but never completely supplanted. Science offers the idea that behavior can be as rigorously studied and brought under laws as the operations of physical or chemical forces. This view is still widespread (for evidence, pick up any recent issue of a public management journal) but remains vulnerable to philosophical critique. However, philosophy has often turned back to Kant despite the gap between his view that reason can lead us to firm conceptual premises and the postmodern view that no such premises are possible.

Interestingly the French theorist Michel Foucault, often cited (despite his objections) as a prominent postmodernist, wrote his own essay titled "What Is Enlightenment?" Though Foucault departs from Kant in many respects, he is more appreciative than critical. Kant is important in Foucault's eyes for describing the attitude of modernity—daring to know. The implication is that modernity is not a period in history but an attitude. It consists in "consciousness of the discontinuity of time: a break with tradition, a feeling of novelty, of vertigo in the face of the passing moment."[28] (Recall Marx's everything solid melts into air.) But modernity is not *just* rupture and vertigo: the modern attitude also aims to recapture "something eternal that is not beyond the present instant, nor behind it, but within it."[29] This does not mean that the present has an essence or inevitability: "The present, in Foucault's work, is less an epoch than an array of questions."[30] It has educative value, if we will only pay attention to it, "imagine it otherwise than it is, and . . . transform it not by destroying it but by grasping in it what it is"—not approving of what is happening but coming to terms with it.[31] Foucault argues that the *attitude* of modernity recognizes *today* as a unique moment in history (not simply different from or the same as yesterday). We must explore the ramifications of this moment—ponder the eventfulness of the event.[32]

For Foucault, Kant's distinction between private (on-the-job) reason properly bounded by authority and public reason, which should never be bounded, raises the philosophical and political question, "How is a public use of reason to be assured?" How can "the audacity to know be exercised in broad daylight[?]"[33] After all, Kant himself was reined in by his king. These questions are particularly pointed in the wake of September 11, 2001, which spurred lawmakers to put in place significant limits on free speech. In light of the Patriot Act, how can members of the public assure themselves that the state will never reach beyond its legitimate limits to encroach on the free exercise of reason in the public world? This is a particularly troubling issue in light of the renewal of the act with most of its original provisions still in place, even though enough perspective on the events was available after four years to make a more balanced approach conceivable.

Foucault urges us to reinvigorate our connection to the Enlightenment, not by slavishly following one or another "doctrinal element" and certainly not by trusting in science and technology, but by heeding Kant's call, *Sapere Aude!* In other words, engage in our own critique of our times. Refuse "Enlightenment blackmail," which is the notion that your only two intellectual choices are either to accept the narrow version of Enlightenment rationalism, in which science and logic are the only respectable forms of knowledge, or to show yourself as totally irrational. There is a third option: move beyond the confines of this either-or forced choice and test "the contemporary limits of the necessary." In doing so, probe the extent to which human actions can be adequately understood as behavior and therefore subject to causal laws or are free in a way that chemicals cannot be.[34] Next, examine your own situation to separate that which is necessary (you can't do anything about it) from that which is subject to change.

In public service this test initially might take the form of skepticism about the notion that somehow the work can be done the right way or the best way, as science seems to promise, rather than being based on judgment and deliberation. The problem with thinking there is a right answer to questions of administration and management is that this perspective gives power to the person or institution that claims to have the answer. Leaving it up to science (for example, performance measurement) is like leaving it up to the ethics commission to say what is right or wrong rather than wrestling with tough questions by reflecting, talking to others, and then doing your best to judge what to do. Believing that not only is there a right answer but that someone in authority can tell you what it is meets Kant's definition of immaturity. The only way to grow in wisdom is to exercise your own intelligence and understanding as best you can rather than leaving it completely up to authority, a person or a rule or a scientific study, to define the right course of action.

As Foucault said, "What is at stake, then, is this: How can the growth of capabilities be disconnected from the intensification of power relations?" How can public servants learn to exercise their public responsibilities and obligations more wisely, without falling into rote application of laws and regulations or the notion that administrative expertise trumps the daily-life knowledge of citizens? Foucault advises us to begin the work of enlightenment by engaging in what he calls a "critical ontology of ourselves." He means develop a critical attitude: observe what people in various practical arenas, including our own, do and the way they do it. What forms of rationality organize the work? What are the intellectual and value assumptions? How do these assumptions shape and limit the actions people take? With what freedom do they act within them?[35]

Both Foucault and Kant, for all their differences, believed that reason could examine itself—its own operations, premises, and blind spots. By daring to know not just about the world but about ourselves, we open up realms of freedom that otherwise would remain forever closed to us. Not that we end up by being able to do anything we want. Daring to know means being able to see "conditions of possibility"—to "separate out, from the contingency that has made us what we are, the possibility of no longer being, doing, or thinking what we are, do, or think."[36]

Public servants can adopt an expanded attitude of modernity—not the one that relies on light/dark, us/them dichotomies, but the one that dares to know. They can reflect on the grounds of their own reasoning. The exercise of reason does not lie in rule following, measurement, or analysis—at least, not in these activities alone. These are only a part of reason and not the most interesting part. As soon as reason examines itself, its limits are revealed because the rules of reason neither exhaust nor limit an individual's free thought and action. They give it shape and guidance but if there were nothing to reason except rule following and the scientific method, exercising it would be a matter of necessity rather than of freedom. The rules would lead us unerringly to the right answer. In this sense thinking for yourself is a leap into the void. There is, finally, a darkness at the heart of reason. It is unable to encompass itself fully, or rather it reaches its limits in the attempt. Being reasonable, then, in the deepest sense consists of accepting the limits of reason. The feeling that "everything seems to be breaking down or in decline, darkening or going under,"[37] such as many people have had since September 11, stems in part from confrontation with the inadequacy of reason in the face of the event. Not just that terrorism is dark, but that the light of reason is not absolute enough to permeate it fully.

There are traces of darkness within every light, and vice versa. The dichotomy can never be made absolute, nor should we try. We must find other avenues to explore to come to terms with September 11. A place to begin is by questioning the gulf that has opened in our own minds between us and them, light and dark, barbarism and civilization. By daring to use our intelligence to explore the situation in which we find ourselves, by refusing to get it right by simply following authorities, we may be able to live, in the most practical way imaginable, a philosophical life.

NOTES

1. Stephen Kinzer and Todd S. Purdum, "An American Debate: How Severe the Threat?" *New York Times*, August 5, 2004, A11.

2. Mark Juergensmeyer, *Terror in the Mind of God: The Global Rise of Religious Violence* (Berkeley, CA: University of California Press, 2003), 5.

3. Jacques Derrida, in Giovanna Borradori, *Philosophy in a Time of Terror: Dialogues with Jürgen Habermas and Jacques Derrida* (Chicago and London: University of Chicago Press, 2003), 153.

4. Juergensmeyer, *Terror in the Mind of God*, 148–49.

5. Peter Berger and Thomas Luckmann, *The Social Construction of Reality* (Harmondsworth, UK: Penguin Books, 1967), 116, 119. Politicians who seek to capitalize, for good or ill, on catastrophes would do well to read Berger and Luckmann, who argue that the institutional order is constantly threatened by chaos. Terrible events like September 11 or Hurricane Katrina "have to be followed at once with the most solemn reaffirmations of the continuing reality of . . . sheltering symbols." (121) The threat of chaos is a perilous tool.

6. H. Gerth & C. Wright Mills, ed. and trans., *From Max Weber: Essays in Sociology* (New York: Oxford University Press, 1958), 155, 350.

7. In the literature of public administration, modernity is typically either taken for granted or pointed to with approval. For a rare critique, see Guy B. Adams, "Enthralled with Modernity: The Historical Context of Knowledge and Theory Development in Public Administration," *Public Administration Review* 52 (1992): 363–73.

8. Karl Marx, quoted in Marshall Berman, *All That Is Solid Melts into Air: The Experience of Modernity* (New York: Penguin Books, 1988), 89.

9. Anthony Giddens, *Modernity and Self-Identity: Self and Society in the Late Modern Age* (Stanford, CA: Stanford University Press, 1991), 3.

10. Ibid., 37.

11. Ibid., 127–31.

12. Zygmunt Bauman, *Society under Siege* (Cambridge, UK: Polity Press, 2002), 12.

13. "U.S. Increasing Surveillance of Canadian Border," *New York Times*, August 21, 2004, A28.

14. Richard Bernstein, "Wedding Vows Can Lock Danes Out of their Homeland," *New York Times*, September 10, 2004, A4.

15. Juan Forero, "In Bolivia's Elitist Corner, There's Talk of Cutting Loose," *New York Times*, August 27, 2004, A4.

16. Craig S. Smith, "France Faces a Colonial Legacy: What Makes Someone French?" *New York Times*, November 11, 2005, A1.

17. Hannah Arendt, "Understanding and Politics," in *Essays in Understanding: 1930–1954*, ed. Jerome Kohn (New York: Schocken Books, 2005), 307–27.

18. Jacques Derrida, "The 'World' of the Enlightenment to Come (Exception, Calculation, Sovereignty)," *Research in Phenomenology* 33 (2003), 35.

19. Roy Porter, *The Enlightenment*, 2nd ed. (Basingstoke, UK, and New York: Palgrave MacMillan, 2001), 5.

20. See Bruce Lincoln, *Holy Terrors: Thinking about Religion after September 11* (Chicago and London: University of Chicago Press, 2003), 59ff.

21. Lincoln, 20.

22. On Medicare actuary Richard Foster, see Robert Pear, "Inquiry Confirms Top Medicare Official Threatened Actuary over Cost of Drug Benefits," *New York Times*, July 7, 2004. On Pentagon procurement official Darlene Druyan, see Leslie Wayne, "Air Force at Unease in the Capital," *New York Times*, December 16, 2004, C1.

23. Of the post–September 11 rhetoric on the terrorist threat, Joan Didion commented: "The possibilities of the Enlightenment vanished. We had suddenly been asked to accept . . . a kind of reasoning so extremely fragile that it might have been based on the promised return of the cargo gods." "Fixed Opinions, or the Hinge of History," *New York Review of Books*, January 16, 2003, 55.

24. Immanuel Kant, "What Is Enlightenment?" in *Kant: On History*, ed. Lewis White Beck (Upper Saddle River, NJ: Prentice Hall, 2001), 3.

25. Kant, "What Is Enlightenment?", 5–6.

26. Kimberly Hutchings, *Kant, Critique, and Politics* (London and New York: Routledge, 1996), 18.

27. The idea that agendas never quite pan out as predicted could, if we chose, point toward putting less effort into crafting them (such as in strategic planning) and giving more attention to process: to the interactions of people as they work together. This theme will return later in the book.

28. Michael Foucault, *The Foucault Reader*, ed. Paul Rabinow (New York: Pantheon, 1984), 38.

29. Foucault, *Reader*, 39.

30. Andrew Barty, Thomas Osborne, and Nikolas Rose, "Introduction," in *Foucault and Political Reason: Liberalism, Neo-liberalism and Nationalities of Government*, ed. Andrew Barty, Thomas Osborne, and Nikolas Rose (Chicago: University of Chicago Press, 1996), 5.

31. Foucault, *Reader*, 41.

32. A fine effort to come to terms with a horrible event is the movie "Elephant," about the Columbine High School shootings. Gus Van Zant, the filmmaker, by resisting the temptation to sensationalize, by sticking to a flat documentary style, enables each member of the audience to come to terms with what happened in his or her own way.

33. Foucault, *Reader*, 37.

34. Ibid., 43.

35. Ibid., 47–48.

36. Ibid., 46.

37. Derrida, "The 'World' of the Enlightenment to Come," 13.

CHAPTER 2

Public Administration and the Question of Torture

OVER THE LAST FEW YEARS THE AMERICAN PUBLIC CONVERsation has raised an unusual question, Does America torture? Not that this topic occupied the attention of the majority for more than a brief period around the time of the revelations about Abu Ghraib. Once the photographs had become familiar, the question of whether United States policy sanctioned torture faded from view for most Americans. President George W. Bush declared flatly, "We don't torture"—as if that settled the question, and for many it seemed to do just that. Others continued to wonder. Perhaps the statement "we don't torture" is simply a definition rather than a factual assertion. In other words, whatever we do doesn't count as torture, so what we *are* doing must be (or must be called) something else.

Behind the president's statement were several documents that had been kept from public view. Eventually, they themselves became revelations. Out of sight, and long before events at Abu Ghraib became public knowledge, Bush administration lawyers had been laboring to construct arguments justifying extreme latitude in the treatment of those captured in the "global war on terror." These arguments focused on techniques of interrogation, conditions of imprisonment, and methods by which the legal system would process prisoners or keep them incarcerated indefinitely.

The conversation about torture and related issues concerning the treatment of detainees at Guantanamo Bay and in secret facilities abroad has not gone away, although the general public has turned its attention elsewhere. On the contrary, the conversation continues, in legal briefs, opinion journals, conference discussions, and books.

Career civil servants may be somewhat more interested in this topic than the typical American (if there is such a person). They are engaged in governing and the conversation is about what government does, can do, should or should not do. But the vast majority of people working in government are not likely to see the question of torture as directly relevant to their duties or the meaning of their lives in public service. Yet there are aspects of the issue that touch directly on the nature of public service and how it is practiced. My purpose here is to raise these questions or at least some of them—to provide food for thought to the public servant who wonders, "I'm never going to torture; I'm never even going to be asked to. So what does this whole issue have to do with me?" The argument will be that torture reveals the link between power and truth in governance. The spectacle of abused bodies in state-sponsored prisons confronts every person who exercises state power with the need to reflect on just how far that power can go—more directly, just how far each of us is prepared to go. The question of torture, then, goes beyond what any particular leader of the executive branch authorizes. It touches the heart of governing.

WHAT IS TORTURE?

What is torture, other than, as we have been told, something Americans don't do? At least since Roman times, the definition has remained remarkably stable. A third-century jurist defined it as "the torment and suffering of the body in order to elicit the truth." In the seventeenth century a civil lawyer said that "torture is interrogation by torment of the body . . . for the purpose of eliciting the truth" about a crime known to have occurred. In the twentieth century, a legal historian defined torture as "the use of physical coercion by officers of the state in order to gather evidence for judicial proceedings." The United Nations Declaration against Torture adopted in 1975, a key reference point in the construction of current arguments for or against torture, says the following:

> For the Purpose of this Declaration, torture means any act by
> which severe pain or suffering, whether physical or mental, is
> intentionally inflicted by or at the instigation of a public official
> on a person for such purposes as obtaining from him or a third
> person information or confession, punishing him for an act he
> has committed, or intimidating him or other persons. It does
> not include pain or suffering arising only from, inherent in or
> incidental to, lawful sanctions to the extent consistent with the
> Standard Minimum Rules for the Treatment of Prisoners.

Despite the tendency over the centuries to expand the application of
the word torture, an enduring feature of its definition has been publicness. Torture is performed by public officials for public purposes.[1]

If publicness has been so central to the understanding of torture,
then it is reasonable to ask how central torture is to our understanding
of the word "public." President Bush's declaration that we don't torture
reflects the American tendency to see ourselves as exceptional—as incapable of the wrongs other nation-states inflict on enemies, foreign
and domestic. In a similar way, people who work in government can
distance themselves from torture by reassuring themselves that their
own exercise of power is different. To think coherently about torture
requires resisting this kind of gut reaction. It requires coming to terms
with the connection between torture and government at a profound
enough level to question the assertion that this is not who we are. In
fact who we are is debatable and, as Senator John McCain once said, the
debate about torture is precisely about who we are. The question is not
an abstract, conceptual one. It goes to the heart of our identity as a
people and as individuals partly defined by nationality. It also goes to
our understanding of how far the grant of legitimacy to government
violence extends. These issues, though thrown into bold relief by the
Bush administration, lie at the heart of any president's exercise of executive power.

The attacks of September 11, 2001, set in motion a detailed examination of the nature of torture within the Bush administration. Because
the United States is bound by domestic statute and international treaty
that prohibit torture, the question raised within the administration was,

"What is it, in fact, that is prohibited?" In immediate terms, how far are military and civilian personnel permitted to go in their efforts to extract information from prisoners? With this question comes another: What type of actions can the United States authorize that will not be grounds for prosecution in the future as war crimes?

The discussion, then, was not about what "we"—the government acting in the name of its citizens—should not do. It was about what can be justified either as legal under existing statute or international agreement, or beyond the reach of such provisions. The thrust of the Bush administration documents is, in effect, to establish the following: Here is what it is OK to do—only a rogue prosecutor or judge could possibly come after you.[2] It is an argument not about what is moral but about what is legal.

JUSTIFYING TORTURE

As is now well known, the boundaries of permissible interrogatory behavior were broadly drawn. In the August 1, 2002, memo from Jay S. Bybee, assistant attorney general to Alberto R. Gonzales, then counsel to the president, the justification of the behavior the government wanted to authorize included three elements: the issue of intention, the nature of severe pain, and the president's authority as commander-in-chief. On the question of intent, the memo interprets the applicable statute to provide that causing severe pain during interrogation is only illegal if the interrogator "specifically intends" to cause it. The memo argues that *knowing* with absolute certainty that severe pain will result is not the same thing as specifically *intending* to cause it. Only if causing severe pain were the foremost goal of the interrogation, rather than a means to the goal, would the selected techniques be illegal. Because interrogations are, by definition, about extracting information, causing severe pain is thereby rendered legal under virtually any interrogation.

This separation of intention from results puts forth a standard for government action that sharply divides ends from means. The end or goal of the interrogation is the extraction of information and the infliction of pain becomes a tool; because pain is not in itself the goal, it is rendered morally neutral. The reflective public servant, conscious

of how few action choices are truly without political or moral dimensions, may well ponder the risks of establishing such a precedent. If the
deliberate infliction of pain can be considered simply the means to an
end, what other administrative tools can ever be ruled out?

To evade existing statute, which defines torture as the infliction of
severe pain, the memo uses a second argument. It attempts to cut,
or at least weaken, the link between torture and pain. The question
becomes, "What does 'severe' mean?" The argument defines severe pain
in such a way that very few techniques qualify as torture and can therefore be ruled illegal. For precedent it reaches into such realms as the
Medicare definition of an emergency medical condition, which speci-
fies "death, organ failure, or the permanent impairment of a significant body function." The memo's argument suggests that severe pain
is the kind associated with these conditions, although it has been
pointed out that none of them is necessarily accompanied by severe
pain. The Medicare provision, of course, has nothing to do with pain;
its intention is to define what type of situation constitutes an emergency and therefore obligates a hospital to provide care regardless of
ability to pay.

In a similar way the memo argues that interrogation techniques that
inflict "prolonged mental harm" only qualify as torture if the interrogator deliberately intends it. The harm must rise to the level of pen-
etrating to the "core of an individual's ability to perceive the world
around him" or "fundamentally altering his personality" in the manner
produced by pushing someone to the brink of suicide, subjecting him
to Russian roulette or a mock execution. A "good faith effort" to avoid
mental harm by consulting with experts or reviewing evidence from
past experience is said by the memo's author to constitute "a complete
defense" to the charge of torture.

The upshot of the memo is to restrict torture to situations in which
the interrogator must have pain rather than information as his or her
primary objective and in which the pain that is caused is so extreme that
"only the most heinous acts" can qualify. This would seem to eliminate
virtually all interrogation methods. However, just to clinch the case, the
argument outlines an extremely broad interpretation of the president's

authority as commander-in-chief. It argues that even though torture is illegal, the commander-in-chief can authorize it. The line of argument is this: Any law that encroaches impermissibly on the president's constitutional war powers is illegal. In war, these powers trump virtually every other consideration so that there is almost no permissible restriction. And we are in fact in a war.

Working backward through these three premises, it is important to note first that the war on terror as defined by the Bush administration is open-ended and unlimited. If, despite this, it qualifies as the sort of war the Constitution refers to when it discusses presidential war powers, this is strong grounds for arguing that the president can exercise extremely broad powers over an indefinite period of time. These powers might be held to include authorizing actions such as torture that would otherwise be illegal. However, even these strong grounds, if they are accepted as such, are not unlimited. Writing for the 6–3 majority in *Rasul v. Bush* (2004), Justice Sandra Day O'Connor declared that the Constitution does *not* hand the president a blank check, even in wartime. (This line of reasoning was extended in *Hamdan v. Rumsfeld* in 2006.) However, if the war on terror is a kind of war that does not meet the Constitutional standard, the check is far from blank. In fact, the extent to which presidential war powers are impervious to challenge is a hotly contested question.

The issue comes down to what sort of war we are in and, therefore, how far the president's discretionary authority extends. It goes to the separation of powers that lies at the heart of the American system of government. To what extent does a war profoundly different from the clash between nation-states justify the expansion of presidential power? President Bush and his allies argued that the war on terror makes virtually unlimited presidential power even more necessary than in a conventional war. Critics wonder whether a war that may conceivably last for decades doesn't require more caution. The president's aggressive expansion of executive power sets a precedent that will beckon to future occupants of the Oval Office. Where is the legal or moral barrier that prevents the extension of government authority into every part of the social and political fabric?

Each new revelation about the Bush administration's national security strategies heated up the debate just as it began to die down. In this sort of atmosphere it is easy to overlook the purpose of the administration's position, which was to construct justifications for actions (including torture and the indefinite detainment of prisoners, including U.S. citizens) the *absence* of which Americans are taught as children makes their country virtually unique among nations.

To make the discussion less abstract, it is important to remember the kinds of actions that have been carried out already at the behest of the U.S. government. There is quite a bit of detailed information available to the public about the treatment of detainees in Afghanistan, in Iraq, at Guantanamo Bay and elsewhere, based on numerous reports released by the Defense Department and prepared by various organizations, as well as thousands of pages of FBI interviews made public through Freedom of Information requests by the American Civil Liberties Union. Documented acts include the following:

> Uniformed servicemen and -women, contract interrogators, CIA employees and people in foreign countries have beaten, maimed, sodomized and killed prisoners held in custody. . . . Prisoners have been kicked and punched, their bones broken. Their heads have been hooded, wrapped in duct tape and smashed. Their flesh has been seared with the chemicals in fluorescent lights. They have been frozen to death, suffocated, hung upside down until dead, starved, electrically shocked and waterboarded. And in few if any of these cases have the victims been individually charged; in none of these instances has evidence, pro or con, been formally presented against the individuals subjected to excruciating pain or death.[3]

Confronted with this list public servants working in what many of them no doubt consider rather routine, even humdrum jobs are likely to draw back in horror at the notion that there is an aspect of their work that is similar at all to such brutal treatment. Yet evidence of the worst that government power can inflict helps to define the structure within which every person who possesses such power exercises it.

THE TICKING BOMB SCENARIO

Once detailed knowledge of torture began to come out, along with Bush administration justifications, the public conversation took a strange turn. It abandoned fact and turned to fantasy. This fantastic thought experiment became known as the "ticking bomb" scenario. There are several sources but the script runs essentially the same. A terrorist has hidden a bomb (sometimes a nuclear bomb, sometimes a chemical or biological weapon). It is set to go off in one hour (sometimes a bit more, but soon). You have captured the terrorist and you know that he knows where the bomb is hidden. If you don't find it, a million (the number varies, but it's always big) people will die. Is it permissible to torture him to get the information?

Charles Krauthammer, one source of the scenario, argues that not only is it justified, it is your duty. He says: "However rare the cases, there are circumstances in which, by any rational moral calculus, torture not only would be permissible but would be required [to acquire life-saving information]. And once you've established the principle, to para-phrase George Bernard Shaw, all that's left to haggle about is the price."[4]

A number of commentators have pointed out flaws in this position. One flaw is the "slippery slope" factor—as soon as you grant that there may be rare situations in which torture is permitted, it can soon become an established practice.[5] Krauthammer's flip comment about haggling over the price is evidence. Once it is agreed that torture is ever justi-fied, then the debate shifts from the right or wrong of torture itself to drawing the line between torture that is okay and torture that is not. And every actual use of it nudges the line farther away from "never" toward "often." As David Luban comments, "Once you accept that only the numbers count, then anything, no matter how gruesome, becomes possible."[6]

Another problem with the scenario is that it makes quite a dubious assumption: that the potential torturer *knows for sure* that the prisoner knows where the bomb is hidden. This is rarely if ever the case. As Elaine Scarry noted, in the first two and a half years after September 11, 2001, the United States detained without access to counsel about five thou-sand foreign nationals who were suspected of involvement in terrorism. Only *three* of the five thousand were eventually charged with terrorist acts, and two of the three were acquitted. This record does not comport with the image of omniscient interrogators. Rather it suggests that interrogators don't know most of the time what a detainee knows; they are simply hoping he or she knows something useful.[7]

Scarry also makes the important point that the person responsible for the anthrax attacks in 2001 has never been found, even though only a "tiny handful" of people could possibly have been able to get hold of the precise strain that was used. She comments that "this is not like finding a needle in a haystack, it's like finding a needle in a bright red pincushion that contains one needle and nineteen straight pins."[8] Yet the government has been unable to do it. Thus the narrative featuring a central character positive about who has the crucial information reads more like the script for a thriller movie than a serious exercise in moral reasoning.

Why is this important? Because the ticking bomb scenario stands out as the most vivid and easily remembered piece of rationalization for torture. People now have in their minds a story that claims to prove that one can't be a purist even about something as bad as torture, and that someday somewhere the time will come when you or I just might have to see it as the lesser of two evils. Exceptions have a way of becoming accepted practices, as every bureaucrat knows. Employees of government agencies are cautious about making exceptions to rules in order to avoid setting new precedents that may be hard to live with later on. An exception that facilitates torture should give them pause.

The scenario also has one significant missing element: the possibility of punishment. If someone makes the tragic choice to illegally inflict severe pain on one person in order to rescue many others, he or she ought to be willing to take the consequences. Otherwise the choice is just too easy. In a well-known essay, Michael Walzer pointed out that sometimes people in public life have to violate the rules without being certain this is the right thing to do. But this choice should have a cost. Walzer called the problem of doing wrong in order to do right "the problem of dirty hands." He argued that public officials who break the law for the greater good can only be considered moral if they know they are guilty—they acknowledge that their hands are dirty and accept punishment.[9] By implying that torture would not only be legal but a moral duty, the ticking bomb scenario lets the torturer off the hook. The specter of a torturer with clean hands should haunt us.

The Bush administration position on the issue of torture—what it is, whether the United States has done it or not, whether it is ever justified—is striking in that many of its prominent players are lawyers and very few if any are philosophers. Perhaps this means nothing more than a large number of lawyers (and a small number of philosophers) are typically found in government. But the particular role certain lawyers have played may be worth reflection. The Bybee memo, for example, was written by lawyers and makes the strongest possible case against legal restrictions on torture. It clearly intends to give the administration the green light for aggressive, even unlimited, measures dealing with detainees suspected of terrorism. There is no discussion whatever of possible legal objections to the case it lays out, a one-sided analysis at best, and a possible violation of the lawyerly norm of balance.

Most professional codes specify neutrality in the provision of information to clients, or at least the obligation to alert them to potential vulnerability from a contending interpretation. Granted it is artificial to imagine that lawyers or other government professionals can somehow hermetically seal off their own perspectives on the issues under their review. The question, rather, is what duty they owe the public as government employees. Richard H. Weisberg argues that professionals who construct rationalizations for acts they know to be wrong prepare the ground for practices like torture. His example is Vichy France during World War II. Lawyers chose to exert themselves finding loopholes and ambiguities in anti-Semitic laws rather than protesting their existence: "As many veterans of Vichy . . . told me, had French lawyers . . . rejected the racial laws, history would have told a different and probably far more benign wartime story than the one France has to live with today."[10]

Torture and Truth

Torture teaches public servants something about truth in public life. In "Truth and Politics," Hannah Arendt argues that rational, scientific, and factual truth is fundamentally at odds with political life. The conflict occurs because the fabric of political life, and the free dialogue it constitutes, are made up of opinion—each person's "the way it appears to me." Every opinion arises from a particular perspective and is shaped by that perspective. Political conversation is made up of varied and conflicting opinions, with each seeking to woo others to its position. In contrast, factual and scientific truth claims to be beyond argument and is therefore fundamentally coercive. Truth, once established, ends debate about whatever it asserts.[11]

Despite the tension between truth and politics, however, factual truth does play a vital role in public life as a counterweight to government lies. Arendt's study of totalitarian government identified official lying as a crucial threat to the public realm, one that can lead to "a complete rearrangement of the whole factual texture—the making of another reality, as it were."[12] To prevent governments, even representative democracies, from reconstructing reality, politics has to avoid treating facts "as the results of some necessary development which men could not prevent and about which they can therefore do nothing." At the same time, politics must not deny facts or try to "manipulate them out of the world."[13]

Truth requires impartiality and disinterestedness. Therefore it can only be sought and found *outside* the political realm. But factual truth is important for informing political opinions, "which can differ widely and still be legitimate as long as they respect factual truth."[14] Thus there are two dangers: first, letting political dialogue float free from its mooring in factual truth and, second, mistaking factual truth for political truth: letting scientific and factual truth take over political dialogue and therefore extinguish it. Political debate can be *informed* by truth established outside politics, but political questions can never be *settled* by reference to truth. They can only be settled by persuasion.

On the whole, career civil servants believe it is their duty to uphold the informative role of factual truth in public decision making to avoid a takeover by sheer self-interest and mutual back scratching. Yet torture reveals the dark side of the reliance on unarguable truth: the relationship between truth and power. This relationship has a long history. The ancient Greeks believed that truth, *aletheia*, came from another realm outside ordinary experience. It was buried, hidden out of sight, waiting to be uncovered. In the Greek legal system, the information extracted from slaves under torture was considered on its face to be the truth. One never knew whether citizens were lying or telling the truth and, besides, citizens were legally immune from torture. Slaves, on the other hand, ordinarily lied, but torture forced them to tell the truth—to reveal knowledge that otherwise would remain hidden. Therefore, if the city wished to know the truth about whether a citizen had committed a crime, the way to find out was to torture his slave—to extract the truth by force.[15]

From this practice has evolved the image of truth waiting out of sight for the requisite actions to reveal it. (Think of the recent TV series that began each episode with the admonition, "The Truth Is Out There.") The truth must be won through effort, especially, according to the ancient Greeks, through force inflicted on the body of the slave. The parallel to current understandings of torture is obvious: The truth is hiding inside the detainee, waiting to be extracted by the infliction of pain. The ticking bomb scenario reflects the sense of certainty on which the ancient Greeks based their use of torture. The truth is, unarguably, inside the person to be tortured. If you want that truth, you must be willing to torture to get it.

Elaine Scarry suggests that "to have great pain is to have certainty; to hear that another person has pain is to have doubt."[16] When you have a toothache, you know you are in pain. But when someone says to you, "My tooth hurts," you wonder "How bad is it, really?" Extreme pain is virtually guaranteed to bring forth some response to the torturer's questions. The certainty of pain, displayed in the bodily reactions of the prisoner, is transferred to what he says. The power of the torturer has "produced" the truth. Thus torture is taken to be a truth-producing mechanism despite the incontestable fact that there are hundreds tortured in the absence of any indication that they actually know something vital and who therefore are almost always incapable of "revealing" it.

The spectacle of the tortured body, from which truth has been extracted, is a reminder that the process of getting to the truth is coercive. It is not usually seen this way; the scientific method is held up as an objective, neutral set of rules that are the opposite of political power, in fact, the redeeming influence on it. The rationality of science reins in the power struggle of politics ("who gets what, when, how").

But another understanding of politics gives a different perspective on the role of truth in public life.

There is political risk in aggressive insistence on the truth, as the scientific method reveals it. Arendt described one side of this dilemma as relying on truth extracted from the body within which it is concealed, even if it is the body of nature. But the other side of the dilemma—letting public life depart completely from any foundation in factual truth—is an equal risk.

Arendt takes the term "dark times" from Bertolt Brecht's poem "To posterity," which recites the terrible events ("the disorder and the hunger, the massacres and the slaughterers") that made the twentieth century so dark. She points out how visible to the public all these events were, yet how difficult to see, "Until the very moment when catastrophe overtook everything and everybody, it was covered up not by realities but by the highly efficient talk and double-talk of nearly all official representatives who, without interruption and in many ingenious variations, explained away unpleasant facts and justified concerns." The light of the public that should clarify events and create space to discuss them has been extinguished by "'credibility gaps' and 'invisible government,' by speech that does not disclose what is but sweeps it under the carpet, by exhortations, moral and otherwise, that, under the pretext of upholding old truths, degrade all truth to meaningless triviality."[17]

What would Arendt make—what should Americans make—of the following, a White House aide's statement to a journalist in 2004?

> The aide said that guys like me were "in what we call the reality-based community," which he defined as people who "believe that solutions emerge from your judicious study of discernible reality. . . . That's not the way the world really works anymore. . . . We're an empire now, and when we act, we create our own reality. And while you're studying that reality—judiciously, as you will—we'll act again, creating other new realities, which you can study too, and that's how things will sort out. We're history's actors . . . and you, all of you, will be left to just study what we do.[18]

This comment fairly crystallizes the view of reality held by the Bush administration leadership, from the president outward: When it comes to governing, facts are comparatively unimportant. What counts are self-confidence and the certainty that the administration is on the right path.

John DiIulio, a policy scholar, painted a similar portrait following his departure from leadership of the faith-based initiative. He tells of hearing many staff discussions but "not three meaningful, substantive policy discussions" during his eight months in the White House. Not only lack of policy-relevant knowledge but lack of interest in acquiring it characterized what he notoriously called the Mayberry Machiavellis, staff "who consistently talked and acted as if the height of political sophistication consisted in reducing every issue to its simplest, black-and-white terms for public consumption, then steering legislative initiatives or policy proposals as far right as possible."[19]

DiIulio's comments address the same period of time when the Justice Department was giving careful consideration to building a rationalized case for the infliction of extreme pain on captives in the war on terror and other departures from the normal boundaries of executive power. While the Mayberry Machiavellis played with smoke and mirrors, looking for the right spin, a darker crew did its own reality reconstruction in secret.

LIVING WITHIN THE TRUTH

Where can public servants find a balance between the positive role truth plays in grounding public debate and the negative role it takes when it coerces public opinion?

In 1965 the Czech writer Vaclav Havel, living under state socialism, recounted a story about the struggle between ideology and immediate reality. Evidently a stone window ledge came loose and fell onto the street below, killing a women walking by. A public outcry followed. Soon an article appeared in the government-controlled press that argued that although falling window ledges were indeed to be deplored, the public's attention would be better focused on "mankind and our prospects for the future." After a period of time a second ledge fell and killed someone else. The public again raised its voice. As Havel observes, "it had understood that the so-called prospects of mankind are nothing but an empty platitude if they distract us from our particular worry about who might be killed by a third window ledge."[20]

Havel's writings dig into what he called "living within the truth." Over and over he criticized the Soviet-style government of Czechoslo-vakia for putting ideological correctness and the demands of the sys-tem over the needs and lives of real human beings. Havel lived and wrote in repressive circumstances where the smallest details of life were under surveillance and diversion from official lines of thought carried real risk. He spent four years in prison because he had spoken out.

The fall of communist regimes in Europe might suggest that the danger of thought- and opinion-manipulation by governments has dis-appeared. Yet what both Havel and Arendt saw as the light shed on pub-lic affairs by free politics continues to be threatened by "ideology, . . . political slogans," "double talk," and "camouflage."[21] Granted the situ-ation in the United States today is far from the level of communist repression. Yet more and more actions on the part of the federal gov-ernment challenge bedrock values like privacy, freedom, and the prohi-bitions against torture and other cruel and unusual punishments.

Havel argued that living within the truth meant refusing to accept the official government version of reality, instead taking small steps to question or oppose it. He offered the example of the greengrocer who for years, almost without thinking, placed official slogans in his shop windows. One day he stops doing so, stops voting in fake elections, starts speaking out at political meetings. One can imagine that the grocer started taking seriously the internal dialogue "between me and myself" that Arendt called *thinking* (see chapter 3).

A similar example from today's paper (as I write) brings the point home. Cliff Berger, of Tarrytown, New York, gets up every morning and checks the web for the latest count of the number of dead in Iraq. Then he sends an email with the current figure to about ninety-five people, asking them to call the White House, tell their friends, do *some-thing* about stopping the war. Then it's off to his job in the medical sup-ply business, car pools, and music lessons. He's just an ordinary guy who's "trying in his small way to . . . puncture the comfortable bubble surrounding the war that's everywhere and nowhere, fought by other people's kids with other people's money. That's why his small protest has the ring of truth, whether you support the war or you don't."[22]

Truth in politics, in public life, comes out of living, out of conversation, out of action. It is not lying hidden in nature, much less within the bodies of prisoners. It questions all official constructions of reality. It depends on human capacities for political dialogue, on a plurality of vantage points, and on inextinguishable human freedom.

Most commentators on the war against terrorism tend to take the public service for granted, if they mention it at all. There have been few reflections on the adequacy of existing guidelines for administrative action—norms such as professionalism, neutrality, and official duty—in times as dark as these. The recovery of political capacity in the contemporary state requires looking beyond these conventional guidelines and images, to the question of truth in dark times. In the next chapter I consider in more depth some means by which public servants may be able to live in truth.

NOTES

1. Edward Peters, *Torture*, expanded ed. (Philadelphia: University of Pennsylvania Press, 1996), 1–3.

2. See the August 1, 2002 memo (widely known as the Bybee Memo) from Deputy Assistant Attorney General John C. Yoo to Alberto Gonzalez, Counsel to the President, in *Torture and Truth*, ed. Mark Danner (New York: New York Review Books, 2004), 108–14. The phrase "rogue prosecutor or judge" is a quote.

3. Karen J. Greenberg, "Secrets and Lies," verbatim *The Nation*, December 26, 2005, 39.

4. Anne E. Kornblut, "He Says Yes to Legalized Torture," *New York Times*, December 12, 2005, Week in Review, 1, 4.

5. For example, see David Luban, "Torture, American Style," *Washington Post Weekly*, December 5–11, 2005, 22–23.

6. David Luban, "Liberalism, Torture, and the Ticking Bomb," *Harper's*, March 2006, 15.

7. Elaine Scarry, "Five Errors in the Reasoning of Alan Dershowitz," in *Torture: A Collection*, ed. Sanford Levinson (Oxford, UK: Oxford University Press, 2004), 281–90.

8. Scarry, "Five Errors" 284.

9. Michael Walzer, "Political Action: The Problem of Dirty Hands," *Philosophy and Public Affairs* 2 (1973): 160–80.

10. Richard H. Weisberg, "Loose Professionalism, or Why Lawyers Take the Lead on Torture," in *Torture: A Collection*, 203.

11. Hannah Arendt, "Truth in Politics," in Hannah Arendt, *Between Past and Future* (Harmondsworth, UK: Penguin Books, 1977), 227–64.

12. Arendt, "Truth and Politics," 253.

13. Ibid., 259.

14. Ibid., 238.

15. Page Dubois, *Torture and Truth* (New York and London: Routledge, 1991).

16. Elaine Scarry, *The Body in Pain: The Making and Unmaking of a World* (Oxford, UK: Oxford University Press, 1985), 7.

17. Hannah Arendt, *Men in Dark Times* (San Diego: Harcourt Brace, 1968), viii.

18. Ron Suskind, "Without a Doubt," *New York Times Magazine*, October 17, 2004, 51. Copyright 2004 by Ron Suskind, reprinted with permission of the Wylie Agency, Inc.

19. *Drudge Report*, December 2, 2002.

20. Vaclav Havel, "On Evasive Thinking," in Vaclav Havel, *Open Letters: Selected Writings 1965–1990* (New York: Vintage Books, 1992), 11.

21. Havel, "Politics and Conscience," in *Open Letters*, 267; Arendt, *Men in Dark Times*, viii.

22. Peter Applebome, "Antiwar Dad Lets Fingers Do Marching," *New York Times*, April 26, 2006, A18.

CHAPTER 3

Thinking, Judging, and Public Life

I N THE PREFACE TO *Men in Dark Times*, HANNAH ARENDT DIS-
tinguished between the kind of horrible event the twentieth century was all too familiar with and another kind of darkness. The
catastrophes were obvious, if not their meaning. Everyone who lived
through them felt their darkness of spirit.

As a German Jew who barely escaped from the impending Holocaust, Arendt knew about terrible events. But her project was greater
than lamenting catastrophes. Instead she pointed to the darkness that
comes when the light of the public realm goes out. Rather when it is
put out, for the light of the public had not somehow faded on its own.
It had been extinguished by the "highly efficient talk and double-talk
of nearly all official representatives who, without interruption and in
many cases ingenious variations, explained away unpleasant facts and
justified concerns."[1]

Her diagnosis and indictment were sharply targeted. The root of the
dilemma was speech by public officials "that does not disclose what is
but sweeps it under the carpet, by exhortations, moral and otherwise,
that, under the pretext of upholding old truths, degrade all truth to
meaningless triviality." (Today's political rhetoric offers many examples
of truths faded into triviality: "family values," "our way of life," or
public administration's favorite—"results.") Despite this profound concern, Arendt did not believe that finding meaning in a dark world was
hopeless. It would come not from "theories and concepts" but "from

the uncertain, flickering, and often weak light that some men and women, in their lives and their works, will kindle under almost all circumstances and shed over the time span that was given them on earth." The source of light would not be leaders of national and global systems but individual lives, and the actions and speech of people whose stories might serve others as "candles" to light the darkness—perhaps, when history came to judge them, as "blazing sun[s]."[2]

The well-known reputation of totalitarian dictators in Nazi Germany, the USSR, and Eastern European satellites for official lying gave force to Arendt's warnings about twentieth-century leaders. The twenty-first century faces a problem other than state terror, or so leaders say today. Totalitarianism is not unknown, but it has given way to the threat of shadowy acts carried out in hidden cells and networks. Nevertheless lessons from a prior century should make people slow to accept what leaders say about the nature of the present danger.

Members of the public are not as alert as perhaps they once were to the risk of accepting official explanations, reassurances, and promises. People are skeptical, to be sure, but the fear of further attacks makes them as vulnerable as ever to official doubletalk. The public is divided when news comes of extended imprisonment without trial and eavesdropping without warrants, practices once considered rare in the United States. Some say such deeds are a threat to the liberty of citizens, many say they are the price we pay for safety. Meanwhile in the public service, turbulent times call for a reexamination of long-established values. This is particularly true of administrative practice in agencies where a multitude of balancing acts between security and liberty are made daily—acts requiring considered judgment.

The first essay in *Men in Dark Times* is Arendt's address upon accepting the Lessing Prize in 1959. She offered Friedrich Lessing, German playwright and leading figure of the Enlightenment, as one of those people whose example can light the darkness for the rest of humanity. He was both radically critical of what was going on in the world and also conscious of his indebtedness to the world. As Arendt observed, "Lessing never felt at home in the world as it then existed and probably never wanted to, and still after his own fashion he always remained committed to it." He lived at the margin—critical of society, but still engaged in it. Arendt attributed this ability to the fact that "he never allowed supposed objectivity to cause him to lose sight of the real relationship to the world and the real status in the world of the things or men he attacked and praised." In contrast to many other Germans, she said, Lessing never confused objectivity with justice.[3]

In public service and particularly in public administration there is a tendency to treat objectivity *as* justice. Science, "the truth," becomes the accepted counterweight to political self-interest and irrationality. This belief is captured, for example, in characterizing policy analysis as speaking truth to power. Science, it is said, enables public servants to speak the objective truth. The idea that objectivity is central to their duty as people charged with governance permeates the literature of public administration and policy, beginning with Woodrow Wilson's claim that expertise in the "eminently practical science of administration" is neutral by definition.[4]

Early municipal reformers, the founders of training in public administration, believed in the power of facts to make governing more rational. In an age when machine politics shaped public life in most large American cities, reformers hoped that scientific objectivity would be an antidote to what they saw as the biggest governance problem of the day: the quid pro quo wheeling and dealing of the machine bosses and their loyalists in administrative agencies. The reformers believed the facts they could dig up about the poor performance of city governments would wake up the public, interest them in government, and throw light on graft and corruption, which operated best in darkness. They believed that getting factual information to the public strengthened democracy.[5] In contrast to Arendt the reformers thought objectivity and justice were pretty much the same thing.

Today those who care about government effectiveness are not as trusting as the municipal reformers were in the redemptive power of facts. But belief in the capacity of scientific objectivity to temper political dynamics has persisted (especially, I would say, among academics). From the maxims of the 1920s and 1930s, such as Luther Gulick's POSDCORB[6], to today's emphasis on following scientific methodologies, the quest continues for true knowledge about what works best. Among public administrators, the search for effective management centers on tools

that Wilson would have included in what he called "practical science":
performance measurement, policy analysis, outcome assessment, and
contract monitoring. Academics and practicing managers argue about
the kind of knowledge practitioners need but rarely about whether
objectivity is important. In the often complex and unstable world of
administrative practice, objective information is seen as a necessary center of gravity, especially when its claims are being buffeted by pressures
from legislators, interest groups, and the general public.

Dark times call on public servants—as well as members of the public—to rethink the connection between what is and what should be. The
darkness of horrific events such as terrorist attacks and devastating
hurricanes requires reflective understanding; no amount of measuring
their impact will enable us to come to terms with them. The darkness
that remains after the light of the public has been put out by official
camouflage and doubletalk will not be relit by facts. Governance requires wisdom, and wisdom requires judgment. This chapter reflects on
these requirements.

TRUTH

Objective information often counts among administrators as one of the
few shreds of sanity in their working lives. To them, Hannah Arendt's
declaration that by the mid-twentieth century the pillars of the best-
known truths lay in ruins can seem rather rude and unwelcome. Arendt
was pessimistic about the potential for speaking truth to power, "The
chances of factual truth surviving the onslaught of power are very slim
indeed; it is always in danger of being maneuvered out of the world
not only for a time but, potentially, forever."[7] Indeed in an essay on the
Pentagon Papers she observed, "Truthfulness has never been counted
among the political virtues, and lies have always been regarded as jus-
tifiable tools in political dealings."[8] Two worrisome tendencies were
the public's vulnerability to distortions, which could be chalked up to
human cognitive limits, and the ability to deny actuality. Confronted
with evidence that we are being lied to, we simply ignore or reject it. Both
make us vulnerable to politicians who aim to obscure what is really
going on.

The difficulty with lying in politics is that lies deal with facts, and facts are never completely unarguable. Therefore separating truth from lying is not a simple technical operation. Facts in political life are based on eyewitness testimony, data, or other evidence. They are not true by necessity, in the way of an equation; rather they are contingent. They depend on how strong the evidence is and what it means. As Arendt saw, the fabric of facts in daily life "is always in danger of being perforated by single lies or torn to shreds by the organized lying of groups, nations, or classes, or denied and distorted."[9] Reality is not as obvious as we often assume. Instead, it is rather a fragile phenomenon that depends on interchanges of various kinds, whether mediated or direct. A great deal of what we routinely classify as "facts" are actually interpretations (decisions about what the evidence means). People notoriously interpret the same data in different ways. The most obvious recent example is the Iraq war. People look at the same data—numbers of soldiers and civilians killed, extent of territory occupied or ceded, opinion polls—and draw opposing conclusions: the war is a disaster, the war is hard work but basically going well, or at least still worth pursuing. Even specialists disagree about what the data mean. Intelligence reports during the run-up to the war conflicted on crucial issues such as the possible connection between Saddam Hussein and al-Qaeda. These conflicting interpretations might be tolerable if politicians did not take advantage of the fragile web of understandings and move from a debatable assertion to outright deception.

Deception works up to a point because "things could indeed have been as the liar maintains they were."[10] But under normal conditions outright lies are eventually exposed by events. Sometimes, though, as the Pentagon Papers showed, analysis of human affairs by professional problem solvers takes the form of cramming reality into a preconstructed theory or worldview, which requires lopping off all the inconvenient aspects that don't fit. This kind of analysis by blunt force is tantamount to lying, because both are attempts to get rid of inconvenient information—taking advantage of the nature of human facts, which might just be otherwise. Arendt refers to this as an "arrogance of mind, an utterly irrational confidence in the calculability of reality." The Vietnam-era problem-solvers "lost their minds because they trusted the calculating power of their brains at the expense of the mind's capacity for experience and its ability to learn from it."[11] When those who have lost their minds in this way occupy positions of power, and use those positions to shape the understandings of the rest of us, the lies they promulgate can last for a very long time—as reflected in the case of Vietnam.

Arendt concludes that what the Pentagon Papers revealed about the U.S. government's approach to Vietnam was not error or miscalculation but downright concealment and falsehood. The government's lies were not aimed at the enemy but at its own people, especially the Congress. There was little information in the Papers that had not already appeared in newspapers and newsmagazines. Yet the government strove vainly to keep the Papers from being published. "Probably," she notes dryly, such efforts "will not be enough to destroy the Republic."[12]

There is an even deeper issue about truth, however, that makes its place in public life problematic. The appeal to facts as if they were just there in nature makes a validity claim, a sort of "this is it whether you like it or not" assertion that is coercive. Such a claim is intended to put its content beyond argument, beyond the need to seek agreement. "The trouble is that factual truth, like all other truth, peremptorily claims to be acknowledged and precludes debate, and debate constitutes the very essence of political life."[13] If we, the people, buy these claims without weighing the evidence for ourselves, we can be easily manipulated. Some claims will turn out to be deceptive, if not outright false. The problem is compounded when, as in recent years, the public does not have access to the evidence on which claims are based. National security threatens to become not only a valid justification for caution in releasing information but also a cloak for deception. And the public has no way of knowing which is which.

Clearly in asserting that scientific truth claims *weaken* political debate Arendt was not suggesting that we surrender public life to the struggle for power and wealth among selfish elites. She believed deeply that humans are fundamentally political beings, for whom involvement in public debate was an irreplaceable activity because it defines who they are in one another's eyes. But if not on truth claims, then on what is public debate to be based? There is another mode of public life. It depends neither on scientific objectivity nor on self-interested competition.

Instead of blindly following science in politics, Arendt recommended *thinking*. Instead of factual truth, she offered *opinion*. Both were necessary aspects of *judgment*, the defining political faculty.

Why do people in public service need to consider these notions? Public administration has always seen rationality as a way of countering self-interest. Scientific findings promise to enable practical managers and analysts to speak truth to power and keep the policy process from becoming utterly debased. But science's truth claims don't simply temper politics, they attempt to rise above it. Instead of working to improve politics, managerial and analytic expertise often wants to trump it. We need a different understanding of the role of truth in public life, a kind of political truth that acts as an opposing force to official double-talk, to the manipulation of evidence and imagery that puts public life into darkness. Public reason requires a mode of truth that has a connection to factual truth without being determined by it. Thinking, opinion, and judgment and their interrelationships offer a different model of public reason than the one grounded in science and logic. Public servants need this model to work through the sort of balancing acts posed by conflicting values such as security and liberty, a tension taken up in detail in subsequent chapters.

"The Wind of Thinking"

The ability to think is something we take for granted, so much so that if told to think one might respond, "But I'm always thinking!" Arendt, however, believed that a certain kind of thinking was rather uncommon.

Thinking that prepares us to judge is different from what scientists do when they experiment. Scientists do think, but in an instrumental way, geared toward gaining verifiable knowledge. In this respect, science stays on the surface of things, on what presents itself to us, gathering evidence to justify conclusions about what *is*. As Arendt said, "Science . . . is but an enormously refined prolongation of common sense reasoning in which sense illusions are constantly dissipated just as errors in science are corrected."[14] Science aims for irrefutable knowledge, findings that "human beings are not free to reject"—they compel us to recognize their correctness.[15] Science is thinking for a purpose, to accomplish an objective. Scientists are driven forward by the urge to know, whether for practical applications or simply out of intellectual curiosity. The urge is fulfilled when the question is answered, when the goal is reached.

In contrast there is a kind of thinking that accomplishes no tangible end result, can only be engaged in by withdrawing from ordinary activity, and is in a sense destructive: "Thinking as such does society little good, much less than the thirst for knowledge, which uses thinking as an instrument for other purposes. It does not create values; it will not find out, once and for all, what 'the good' is; it does not confirm but, rather, dissolves accepted rules of conduct."[16] The skeptic in us exclaims, Then why on earth do it!

There is a capacity of the mind that abandons accepted rules of conduct, traditional standards, whatever "they" say must or must not be the case, and looks at events and situations in a fresh, critical light. Standardized codes, such as codes of professional ethics, protect us against reality by letting us leap to conclusions that maintain our stability. Right away, when something disturbing happens, we categorize it; we know immediately what it is. But thinking that prepares the ground for political judgment is destabilizing because it "interrupts all doing."[17] Thinking starts with experience; the aim, however, is not to determine its cause but to question its meaning. Thinking circles around events and situations, holds up one or another aspect to a critical gaze, and tries out various interpretations. Arendt characterized it as a conversation between me and myself.

The difficulty with thinking like this is that the deeper one gets into it, the slipperier the concepts get. Words like justice and happiness—even a simple word like "house"—are frozen thoughts that thinking unfreezes. Their meaning shifts and "everything begins to move."[18] It is in this sense that thinking is destructive. Confronted by a perplexing or disturbing event (the September 11 attacks, perhaps, or the deeds done in our names in Abu Ghraib, or the profound government failure after Hurricane Katrina), we try to apply various frameworks such as established moral rules or stories from history, but they don't seem to fit. The "wind of thinking . . . has shaken you from your sleep and made you fully awake and alive."[19] But you seem to be left with nothing to express but questions and quandaries, and nothing to do but share them with others. (Sharing them turns out to be important, as we will see below.)

Thinking, then, doesn't do society any good in the usual sense of producing results. But it might be vital when everyone around you seems to be in the process of being swept away by nonthinking—when no one else seems to be looking hard at something you find troubling, when everyone seems to be hanging on to the tried and true moral rules that you sense are missing the point. In this sense, thinking "asserts the claims of conscience."[20] In fact, by clearing away the old nostrums, thinking does accomplish one thing at least: it prepares you to exercise the power of judgment. And this might be exceedingly important in those "rare moments when the chips are down."[21]

OPINION: THE "IT APPEARS TO ME"

Opinion is important because politics is not about factual truth. Truth compels our assent, whereas politics is made up of argument, debate, and courting the agreement of others. In political argument, factual truth "has a despotic character," because logically it compels agreement. In Arendt's eyes, truth is "domineering" because it needn't take people's opinions into account, and "taking these into account is the hallmark of all strictly political thinking."[22] This does not mean that factual truth has no role whatever to play. Quite the contrary, Arendt believes that "facts inform opinions, and opinions, inspired by different interests and passions, can differ widely and still be legitimate as long as they respect factual truth."[23] But because facts are subject to interpretation, their meaning is often in dispute; the implication is not that facts can mean anything we say but that political argument is often occupied with debating what the facts mean.

To many people in public life, opinion has a rather indecisive, irrational feel to it. We tend to regard it as whimsical or prejudiced, not based on reason or evidence. People's opinions are often thought to be beyond reach. "Well, that's my opinion" tends to be a conversation stopper—a signal that I'm holding on to my viewpoint and nothing you can say is going to change it. Yet many times opinions are not fixed but completely subject to manipulation. So-called opinion polls can produce widely varying results on the same issue by framing the question in different ways. A good example of this occurred in the old days of welfare policy; when asked whether the government should help people in poverty, a majority said yes; but when asked whether the government should be providing "welfare" benefits, most people said no. Whether fixed or flimsy, then, opinion seems an untrustworthy rock on which to ground the political process.

Nevertheless, opinion writ large is a constitutive feature of political life. According to Arendt, its importance comes from the uniqueness of each person. Each birth, each new person is a beginning, the emergence of something completely distinctive into the world. The world "appears"—presents itself to me—differently than it does to any other person. Opinion, therefore, is not "subjective fantasy and arbitrariness, but also not something absolute and valid for all. . . . The world opens up differently" to every person, according to that person's position in it and opinion is "the formulation in speech . . . of what appears to me."[24] Each person's opinion, then, is irreplaceable. The coming together of each person's "it appears to me" makes the political world. This interweaving of the considered opinions of differing people makes up *political* truth.

It is possible that opinion has had a rather lowly status among intellectuals because both philosophy and science, in their respective ways, have sought to get beyond appearance to the "really real." Yet opinions are the crucial building blocks of political reality. This does not mean that each of us should assume the validity of our own opinions without further checking. One of the functions of thinking is to engage in an inner dialogue with myself in order to examine the basis of my opinion. But the ultimate way of testing my own opinion is to enter into dialogue with others, "Nobody can know by himself and without further effort the inherent truth of his own opinion. . . . Talking something through . . . reveals [opinion] in its own truthfulness."[25] Opinion is grounded, then, in two ways: first, thinking, or the silent conversation between me and myself. In this silent talk I determine whether I am in agreement with myself and I consider how the world might seem to me if I were standing in someone else's shoes (more about this below). Second, I enter into conversation with others to know directly how the world seems to them by hearing what they say. Here I test the soundness of my own views.

The notion that persuasion, the exchange of opinions in dialogue, is too risky a foundation for politics dates back to Plato. After the Athenian populace demanded the death of Socrates, Plato (contravening Socrates' own practice) concluded there had to be absolute standards of validity to settle political arguments and keep citizens from deteriorating into a mob. This need for absolute standards is widely felt today. Analysts and management scientists hope to produce unarguable results that will settle political questions. Others hope for similar results by importing the word of God into politics. As numbers of critics have argued, the turn to a higher authority, whether offered by experts, philosophers, or clerics, is a turn away from democracy. Arendt expressed this turn as the loss of the common world, "which would at once relate and separate" people. Without that world, each of us lives "in desperate lonely separation" or becomes an indistinguishable part of a mass.[26]

Judging without Banisters

The third building block in public reason is judgment. One way to approach Arendt's rather complex view of judging is to place it in the context of her life. In 1963 she published *Eichmann in Jerusalem*, perhaps her most widely known work. After attending the trial of Adolf Eichmann, one of Hitler's top administrators, she rendered a judgment of Eichmann's participation in implementing the final solution. His trial defense amounted to the argument that he was following orders, simply doing his duty as a civil servant. Eichmann even maintained that *not* carrying out the orders he was given, to see that all the Jews of Europe were killed as quickly and expeditiously as possible, would have been immoral. Famously, Arendt used the term "the banality of evil" to make the point that, in following an ostensibly moral precept—"duty"—Eichmann's actions resulted in evil even though he maintained that he never intended it. The importance of the Eichmann example for Arendt was not that there is "Eichmann in all of us," a notion she roundly denied. Rather, Eichmann represented the modern tendency to judge automatically, thoughtlessly, according to existing rules and norms, or "banisters."[27]

The book triggered a storm of protest. Some people objected to the idea that Eichmann might not be innately evil (whatever one might mean by that). Others disliked Arendt's harsh criticism of certain Jews who, under extraordinary duress, cooperated with the Nazi regime in various ways. Later Arendt said that the questions she was most often asked were, Who was she to judge, not having been in the situation at the time? How did she know that she herself would not have done the same? Her reply: If we could not judge events at which we were not present, there would be very little we *could* judge. To judge someone's actions as wrong did not at all imply that one might not have done the same thing. Arendt concluded that today there is a "widespread fear of judging." It reflects the tendency to see ourselves as caught up in situations in which we are not free to choose what to do. Furthermore, there is the inclination to assume that we're all equally bad, and anyone who tries to pretend otherwise is either a saint or a hypocrite.[28]

Judging is at the center of politics because politics deals with the unheard of, the unprecedented, the debatable. It can't rely on scientific truth, standardized codes of conduct, or established (therefore taken-for-granted) values as ultimate grounding. These "banisters" support people as they move through life, but they are antithetical to politics, which entails differing opinions and persuasion. Public life is the exchange itself, not the results. As soon as an argument is resolved, politics is at an end, at least for the time being. Judgment guides political dialogue without forcing it to conform to an inappropriate truth standard that would restrict free exchange, which is vital to keep the political dialogue open. In this openness lies our freedom.

Even without absolute standards, such as the rules of scientific method or professional ethics codes, by which public questions can be definitively resolved, this does not mean that anything goes. The coherence of public space depends on the exercise of judgment. Reason is not made "to isolate itself but to get into community with others."[29] Allowing our thoughts to be weighed by others, and assessing their viewpoints in turn, leads to an enlargement of one's own mind and offers the only sort of validity consistent with political freedom—the kind that comes from "testing that arises from contact with other people's thinking."[30]

Judgment deals with "phenomena . . . head-on, without any preconceived system."[31] Arendt suggested that political issues are like works of art people assess for their beauty, because neither politics nor art can be referred to an objective standard or principle. Yet they can be made meaningful.

Judging, then, proceeds something like this. Presented with a dilemma or problematic situation, you first draw upon your imagination to pursue a tentative answer to the question posed by the new: what is this to me? You try to put yourself in the place of as many others in the situation as possible: *not* to empathize with them or to figure out how they feel ("feel their pain"), but to imagine how you would feel if you were standing in their shoes. Arendt called this "training the imagination to go visiting."[32] By doing this you can compare your initial view of the situation and what to do about it with the possible viewpoints of others, based on their various involvements. This move, among other things, is a way of setting aside your own self-interest by testing how your existing viewpoint holds up when your circumstances change. The more possible viewpoints you consider in your imagination, the more likely you are to reach impartiality—not, by the way, a higher standpoint that trumps all the others and settles the matter but a sort of generality from particulars.

The second phase of judging is reflection. Consider your findings or the results of your efforts to imagine how you would feel in others' shoes and the positive or negative sensibilities that arose in doing so. Imagination makes the absent present and gives a fresh sense of the issue, one that pleases you because it feels right or fitting, or doesn't. But what do you do with this pleasure or displeasure? Can you trust it, or not? This is the most difficult part of the process because it approaches the question of whether your imaginings have given you a valid take on the situation. You have done the work of imagining and the results—your new perspective on the situation—have given you an aesthetic sense of fitness or lack of fit. But how to decide whether that sense is the right one?

There are no rules (no banisters) to cling to and therefore guarantee the validity of your judgment. But that doesn't leave you completely at sea. The reason is that judging always takes place in a community, either implied or actual. You developed your new appraisal of the situation out of your experience, education, practice, culture, and so on, and these in turn have been developed in myriad relationships with others. These relationships have made you sensitive to various aspects of situations. The final step in coming up with a valid judgment is to appeal to the community sense by courting the agreement of others. You cannot force their agreement, only try to persuade them by appealing to their own faculty of judgment. As Arendt says, "[Art] and politics, then, belong together because it is not knowledge or truth which is at stake, but rather judgment and decision, the judicious exchange of opinion about the sphere of public life and the common world, and the decision about what manner of action is to be taken in it, as well as to how it is to look henceforth, what kinds of things are to appear in it."[33]

The appeal to others, of course, constitutes your "it appears to me," or your *opinion*; not one that you have fired off from the top of your head, but one you have considered carefully. Still it is possible that when you communicate with others this appeal of yours will be met with a resounding chorus of disagreement. This happened to Arendt herself with the Eichmann book. If your best efforts to woo the agreement of others fail, there is nothing more to do but accept the fact of disagreement or perhaps reconsider your own opinion. For those who would like to resolve disagreements once and for all by appealing to some transcendent standard like equality or the Golden Rule, this lack of resolution is difficult to accept. But it is exactly the lack of closure that makes this way of judging so important for politics because, in contrast to science or logic, it is noncoercive: agreement is either freely gained or not possible at all. Without this freedom, politics disappears.

To sum up briefly, *thinking*, the silent conversation between me and myself, provides critical reflection on the dilemma at hand. The wind of thought clears away the taken-for-granted nostrums and the leaps to conclusions that others have made and are busy making. The results of thinking prepare the way for *judging*, in which imagining how the world appears from other viewpoints makes it possible to put forward a considered *opinion*, to which others may or may not be wooed. This entire process provides a more complex form of public reasoning than the more familiar linear rationality of science and analysis. Arendt was certainly not opposed to the use of reason in public life; she simply wanted a more commodious understanding of it, one that would enable us to attain the kind of validity that kept the door open to politics—to the free exchange of unforced, considered opinions of free citizens. She viewed opinion as "one of our primary rational faculties," but one that renounced "the tyrannizing claim to a singular moral or political truth."[34] Politics is enacted in a public world brought into being by the interchange of unique viewpoints. Therefore it needs a form of reasoning that enables us to reach considered but still free judgments, ones that are valid in the only way consistent with an open public space.

How does this model of public reason mesh with the one considered in chapter 1? Both reject the kind of narrow rationality that restricts the free play of the mind and depends on established rules and codes. Political reasoning depends on a willingness to "dare to know." Scientific method is important in its place but is not an ultimate ground for public life because it leads to facts rather than freedom. Free political dialogue does not lead unerringly to right answers. The only kind of reason that makes free politics possible is the kind that is conscious and accepting of its limits, the kind that recognizes that the source of validity in the debate lies in the process itself and not in an external standard.

Once I heard an expert from a prestigious university try to persuade members of neighborhood councils in Los Angeles that they should measure their efforts by the results—for example, whether they were successful in getting the city to provide certain facilities or services. Fortunately, others countered with the notion that nothing measures the value of the involvement of citizens in public life except the sheer existence of the world they bring into being as they talk with each other and with city officials. As Arendt said, there is a profound difference between acting "in order to" and "for the sake of." One involves the pursuit of goals, the other the pursuit of meaning. Thinking and judging make possible the exchange of considered opinions that constitute meaningful public life, regardless of results. We must light the darkness of dark times in the only way open to us: by rekindling the light that shines only in public conversation.

NOTES

1. Hannah Arendt, *Men in Dark Times* (San Diego: Harcourt Brace & Co., 1968), viii.

2. Arendt, *Men in Dark Times*, viii–x.

3. Ibid., 5–6. Lessing exemplified the practice of what Kant called "public reason" (see chapter 1). His writing spoke out in favor of religious tolerance and other Enlightenment principles. See, for example, his verse play *Nathan the Wise*.

4. Woodrow Wilson, "The Study of Administration," *Political Science Quarterly* 2 (1887), 197–222.

5. See Camilla Stivers, *Bureau Men Settlement Women: Constructing Public Administration in the Progressive Era* (Lawrence, KS: University Press of Kansas, 2000).

6. POSDCORB stands for planning, organizing, staffing, directing, coordinating, reporting, and budgeting, Gulick's list of executive functions. See "Notes on the Theory of Organization," in *Papers on The Science of Administration*, ed. Luther Gulick and Lyndal Urwick (New York: Institute of Public Administration, 1937), 3–13.

7. Hannah Arendt, "Truth and Politics," in *Between Past and Future: Eight Exercises in Political Thought* (Harmondsworth, UK: Penguin Books, 1977), 231.

8. Hannah Arendt, "Lying in Politics," in *Crises of the Republic* (San Diego: Harcourt Brace & Co., 1972), 4.

9. Arendt, "Lying in Politics," 6.

10. Ibid.

11. Ibid., 39. Parallels between the way U.S. leaders handled the Vietnam War and the way they have handled the Iraq War are worth pondering. That one group of leaders was Democratic and the other Republican shows that party affiliation is no insurance against doubletalk and camouflage.

12. Ibid., 47.

13. Arendt, "Truth in Politics," 241.

14. Hannah Arendt, *The Life of the Mind: One: Thinking* (San Diego: Harcourt Brace & Co., 1978), 54.

15. Arendt, *Thinking*, 59.

16. Hannah Arendt, "Thinking and Moral Considerations," in *Responsibility and Judgment*, ed. Jerome Kohn (New York: Schocken Books, 2003), 188.

17. "Thinking and Moral Considerations," 164.

18. Ibid., 170.

19. Ibid., 175.

20. Dana Villa, "The Banality of Philosophy," in *Hannah Arendt Twenty Years Later*, ed. Larry May and Jerome Kohn (Cambridge, MA: MIT Press, 1996), 179.

21. Arendt, "Thinking and Moral Considerations," 189.

22. Arendt, "Truth and Politics," 241.

23. "Truth and Politics," 238.

24. Hannah Arendt, "Philosophy and Politics," *Social Research* 57 (1990), 80. Originally published 1954.

25. Arendt, "Philosophy and Politics," 81.

26. Hannah Arendt, "The Concept of History," in *Between Past and Future* (see note 6), 89–90.

27. Hannah Arendt, *Eichmann in Jerusalem* (New York: Viking Press, 1963). See also Villa, "The Banality of Philosophy," 184; and Lawrence J. Biskowski, "Practical Foundations for Political Judgment: Arendt on Action and World," *Journal of Politics* 55 (1993), 867–87.

28. Hannah Arendt, "Personal Responsibility under Dictatorship," in *Responsibility and Judgment* (note 15), 17–48.

29. Hannah Arendt, *Lectures on Kant's Political Philosophy*, ed. Ronald Beiner (Chicago: University of Chicago Press, 1982), 40.

30. Arendt, *Lectures*, 42.

31. Arendt, quoted in Lisa Jane Disch, *Hannah Arendt and the Limits of Philosophy* (Ithaca, NY and London: Cornell University Press, 1994), 145. Disch's discussion provided significant help to me in sorting out Arendt's views on judging.

32. Arendt, *Lectures*, 43.

33. Hannah Arendt, "The Crisis in Culture," *Between Past and Future* (note 6), 223.

34. Dana Villa, *Politics, Philosophy, and Terror: Essays on the Thought of Hannah Arendt* (Princeton, NJ: Princeton University Press, 1999), 80.

PART II

Two Models of Governance

CHAPTER 4

There's No Place Like Homeland: Security in Dark Times

B Y THE SUMMER OF 2005, THE EVENTS OF SEPTEMBER 11, 2001, the wars in Afghanistan and Iraq, and revelations concerning Abu Ghraib and Guantanamo had all combined to produce a palpable sense of living in dark times. Questions of homeland security had become central to governance. Then Hurricane Katrina slammed into the coasts of Louisiana and Mississippi, virtually destroying New Orleans and many smaller communities along the Gulf Coast. Although arguments continued long afterward about the adequacy of federal, state, and local emergency response, in the minds of many Americans government had failed its most basic responsibility: to help its citizens in a time of dire need and to protect them from further harm.

This horrifying series of events opened fissures in people's understandings of homeland security. A couple of years earlier, Donald Kettl had argued that "homeland security, at its core, is about coordination. . . . The key to an effective homeland security system is, in fact, connecting the dots—ensuring strong coordination among those responsible for prevention and those charged with response."[1] People who study and practice administration often take the view, perhaps only half-consciously, that if only the right formula for organizing work and assigning responsibility can be found, things will fall into place and everything will run smoothly—or, at least, more so than before. Many of the post-Katrina criticisms leveled at governments have centered on failure to coordinate rescue efforts. These charges reflect the continuing belief in the power of the right system. Certainly they mark the belief that there *is* a right system.

Without swallowing the coordination nostrum whole, when it comes to figuring out how a problem should be tackled or a job done better, people who write about public administration often recommend reorganizing. Faith in reorganizing persists, despite the fact that a mountain of research over the years has failed to turn up convincing evidence that it actually does help agencies work better. In an often-cited review, James March and Johan Olsen found that "few efficiencies are achieved; little gain in responsiveness is recorded, control seems as elusive after the efforts as before." They concluded that reorganization acts a symbol—"ritual confirmation of the possibility of meaningful individual and collective action."[2] Public leaders want to be seen as taking decisive action to prevent a particular disaster from recurring. Moving the boxes around on the organization chart is relatively easy to do and highly visible. It sends a signal that leaders can deliver on their promise to fix problems. Changing the established patterns of action for which the organization chart is shorthand, however, is another matter.

A few months after September 11, 2001, one seasoned manager wrote that managerial turbulence in the wake of the creation of the Department of Homeland Security would reduce for years the effectiveness of the agencies involved, divert the Homeland Security secretary's attention from strategic to routine administrative matters, and prevent him from mobilizing and using political clout. This senior bureaucrat quoted managerial advice from Petronius Arbiter in the third century BC, "We tend to meet any new situation by reorganization, and a wonderful method it can be for creating the illusion of progress while producing confusion, inefficiency, and demoralization."[3]

If reorganization doesn't actually deliver the goods we hope it will, why do we continue to resort to it? In the case of September 11, the pressure on government leaders to do something visible was irresistible. Together with the rather ill-defined idea that behind our vulnerability to the September 11 attack lay a failure to "connect the dots," this pressure pushed legislators and executive officials inexorably toward doing something plausible, something that seemed to have at least a chance of making us safer. The same impetus must surely have driven the creation of the post of intelligence czar, despite warnings from a number of experts that it was not a particularly good way of streamlining intelligence operations.

Most of the commentary on the government response to Katrina has also emphasized reorganizing. Causes of the breakdown have been identified as communication failures, information gaps, and lack of coordination across agencies and levels of government. A veteran observer cautioned against putting too much faith in strategies that will make the structures of government even more complex, "I fear the current trend . . . is to build more boxes within which people are constrained to operate."[4] Yet government failures continue to be chalked up to structural flaws. A snowstorm in February 2007 left hundreds of motorists and truckers stranded on several Pennsylvania highways for two days. Backups in some places were fifty miles long. At a press conference, Governor Edward Rendell said there had been a communications breakdown among agencies and ordered a review.[5]

The need to do something, or at least appear to be doing something, is completely understandable and a long-standing feature of American political life. But as Dwight Waldo once said, in public administration people have a tendency to set their sights on the superficial—that is, they try to solve immediate problems without reflecting on deeper dimensions. Whatever else our leaders decide to do, no matter how effective or ineffective the results, homeland security has assumed enormous proportions in our public life. Americans, especially those whose working lives put them in strategic positions in public life (and that now includes virtually anyone working in government at any level), need a source of stability for the decisions and practices that make up the fabric of governance. Otherwise we remain vulnerable, not only to terrorist attack and other unexpected disasters, but to being caught up and swept along in ideological tides not of our making. Currently accepted ideas about security are a less meaningful anchor for governance than others that might come to light upon reflection.

SECURITY IN THE HOBBESIAN DECADE

After Hurricane Katrina hit, commentators on both ends of the political spectrum agreed that its devastation had profoundly affected American public sensibilities. Conservative columnist David Brooks worried about the "thin veneer of civilization, the elemental violence in human nature . . . the uncertain progress good makes over evil." His diagnosis concluded, "It's already clear that this will be known as the grueling decade, the Hobbesian decade."[6] From the liberal side, Paul Krugman charged that the Bush administration's "ineptitude" at dealing with the disaster "was a consequence of ideological hostility to the very idea of using government to serve the public good."[7]

Brooks's reference to philosopher Thomas Hobbes was far from idle. To Hobbes we owe the idea that providing security from internal and external threats is the bedrock responsibility of the state. It is the one function for which even the most antigovernment commentator is ready and willing to grant the need. In Hobbes's thinking, security is fundamental because without it society itself is not possible. He argues that the natural condition of humankind is war, either actual fighting or simply the threat that it will break out at any minute. In one of the most famous passages of Western political theory, Hobbes says that in this natural condition

> There is no place for Industry; because the fruit thereof is uncertain; and consequently no Culture of the Earth; no Navigation, nor use of the commodities that may be imported by Sea; no commodious Building; no Instruments of moving, and removing such things as require much force; no Knowledge of the face of the Earth; no account of Time; no Arts; no Letters; no Society; and which is worst of all, continuall feare, and danger of violent death; And the life of man, solitary, poore, nasty, brutish, and short.[8]

Hobbes is widely considered to be the de facto founder of a realist school in political thinking. This realism, rooted in a view of human nature as essentially violent, is widely shared. Contemporary Americans view as plain common sense the idea that when all is said and done "all men, old or young, big or small, famous and rich or poor and unknown, have more or less equal capacities to kill each other,"[9] as well as the propensity to do so if not checked in some way. To base a theory of public life on man's inherent violence seems realistic and certainly safer than assuming that people are basically good and trustworthy.

The crux of realism, however, is not just assuming that people are essentially selfish and violent, but that because of this essential element in human nature, basing policy on considerations of right and wrong, just and unjust, is woolly-headed and foolishly risky.[10] Better to assume the worst about people and act accordingly. Carried to its logical conclusion, this view excuses any kind of behavior that can somehow be justified as necessary for security: "Realism's bracing promise is to spring politics free from the constraints of moral judgment and limitation . . . and to offer a picture of the world of people and states as they really are rather than as we might yearn for them to be. . . . Realist thinkers exude the confidence of those whose narrative long ago 'won the war.' . . . Alternatives [are] cast into a bin labeled idealism that, for the realist, is more or less synonymous with dangerous if well-intentioned naivete."[11]

Americans (like most other Westerners in this regard) are so used to interpreting political life along these lines that it is difficult to introduce the possibility of an alternative. In my experience this is the most difficult assumption to get public administration classes to reexamine, particularly when the only alternative they can think of is basic altruism, which seems clearly untenable to them. Nearly all my students are working in the public sector and they place a very high value on practicality, which is the form their realism takes. Many are so sure that people are basically selfish, and would be violent if left to their own devices, that they have developed a real flair for interpreting all behavior of whatever kind in these terms—even sacrificing one's life for another.

During Hurricane Katrina, observers readily accepted news reports of violence on the part of residents struggling to survive; these accounts were greatly exaggerated or entirely groundless. Reports of gang rapes, dead children abandoned on the floor of the convention center, and so on all turned out to be false. Hundreds of bodies were said to be stashed in the basement of the Superdome; when a doctor showed up to process them, saying he had been told there were two hundred, it turned out there were six: one drug overdose, one suicide, and four deaths from natural causes. Federal relief efforts were diverted and delayed out of a belief that the whole city was unsafe. A veteran journalist commented that the portrait in many newspaper accounts was of "a city gone mad, a black city, a city of depraved men and women."[12] The question is, why were such rumors so readily disseminated and so widely believed?

Reports of this kind are fed by assumptions about the natural violence of humanity (not to mention, in the case of New Orleans, racism). To understand the source of these bedrock beliefs, it is important to look in a bit more detail at what Hobbes himself said, to reveal the downside of the bargain he laid out between subjects and the sovereign. There is another way of thinking about security, one that brings our attention to more productive understandings.

Hobbes

Hobbes starts with the view that the "generall inclination of all mankind" is "a perpetuall and restlesse desire of Power after power, that ceaseth only in Death."[13] Only by continuing to seek more power can one ensure not losing the power one already has and with it the means to live well. But beneath the ceaseless struggle for power is man's awareness of his mortality. This awareness is the source of constant anxiety, "a perpetuall solicitude of the time to come. . . . So that man, which looks too far before him, in the care of future time, hath his heart all day long, gnawed on by feare of death, poverty, or other calamity; and has no repose, nor pause of his anxiety, but in sleep." "Perpetuall feare" is the real source of human longing for security, "always accompanying mankind in the ignorance of causes, as it were in the Dark." Unable to explain life and fate to themselves, constantly vulnerable to violence, human beings seek to be secure and to feel secure by agreeing with their fellow humans to live under the authority of a state, and by turning to religion, positing some invisible cause to explain what happens, "In which sense perhaps it was, that some of the old Poets said, that the Gods were at first created by human Feare."[14]

Anxiety and fear in the face of uncertainty and under threat of attack lead human beings to turn to authority to calm fears and settle disputes. This authority is most obviously embodied in law and the state's grant of legitimacy to exercise violence but also in institutions like science and religion that claim to have ultimate answers—to speak authoritatively.

Despite authorities, however, the "radical uncertainty" of the human condition cannot be expunged because what we fear most is nameless, "An objectless fear is an unresolvable fear. No one can fight or flee what he cannot identify or know. To be resolvable, fear must attach to something; it must have an object. Thus when an object is lacking, men will find an imaginary one."[15] In this sense, the figure of the terrorist is made to order for feeding people's otherwise wordless fears. The terrorist symbolizes the ultimate riskiness of life, the vulnerability to attack that can never be eliminated. Not that terrorism isn't a real threat; indeed, its reality is what makes it a powerful symbol. People can't be soothed, as children are about monsters under the bed, with reassurances that there's nothing there. One day there might be. So instead of coming to terms with life's fundamental uncertainty, and the need for resoluteness in the face of it, we turn our fear toward something explicit in the hope that some system or other will rescue us.

Because other animals are equally if not more violent, it is not violence that makes us human but self-awareness, language, and culture. If we fight, if we have different ideas about the good, we can still agree not to tear each other apart. According to Hobbes, what saves humans from the war of all against all is that we develop institutions. Institutions are the product of human agreements about what ends and practices to value. Because they are human constructions, we can know them completely. We can study their workings and develop a "civil science" that will give us the only possible certainty and the findings of which can be taught. Hobbes's idea of a civil science is the seed from which much of the study of public life has sprung, and the prospect of certain knowledge about the workings of political and administrative institutions remains immensely attractive to many. But two problems persist.

The first problem is that civil science carries a price tag that is often overlooked. In Hobbes's state, for the sake of security, politics has been removed from the life of society and turned over to the sovereign—to Leviathan. The frontispiece to the 1651 edition of Hobbes's classic depicts Leviathan as a giant looming over a city, sword in one hand, scepter in the other. The body of the giant is made up of countless tiny human beings, but the head of the sovereign is unitary. The people make up the strength and sinews of Leviathan, but his head does all the thinking. We have resolved our differences from one another by turning the decision making over to him.

In Hobbes's state, citizens will be educated to the wisdom of confining their ambitions to private desires and leaving public choices up to authority—first of all to Leviathan but backed up by the authority of science. If they could not learn this, avoiding the war of all against all would be hopeless. Diverse opinions, which cannot be resolved, and the bellicose actions they would likely produce, are dealt with by getting rid of all opinion. The only political actor is the sovereign, whether a monarch or a lawmaking body. Peace is purchased at the cost of politics—leaving legislation and execution up to those in authority. Individual opinions are bad not only because they cause strife but also because governing must be left to those who are really in the know—the "civil scientists."

> Hobbes believed that education would enlighten people by giving them foresight—'those prospective glasses'—to see and feel the terrible consequences of . . . vanity . . . without having to experience them directly. *The purpose of enlightenment is to make human beings who are secure feel insecure.* . . . The price of objective security is subjective insecurity. . . . If you 'enjoy' your security, then you will take it for granted. . . . But if you feel insecure, if you feel in your bones 'the continuall fear, and danger of violent death,' then you will continually cherish peace and the state that provides it.[16]

In contrast to the notion of enlightenment as the maturity to think for oneself, Hobbes's idea is to instill enough fear in people so that they will refrain from thinking for themselves—from forming the considered opinions necessary to authentic public life. If citizens expressed opinions, the risk to the state's stability would be great.

In Hobbes's state the cost of security is high, at least for the ordinary citizen. What we trade for security is, first, participation in politics and, second, the hope of *feeling* secure, for if we feel secure, our willingness to turn over power to authority diminishes. We might begin to feel that we could handle public affairs better ourselves. This would be a fatal mistake, because sooner rather than later the war of all against all would break out. The stability of the Hobbesian government lies in the people's obedience. Whether they live in a monarchy, an aristocracy, or a democracy, the people flourish because they obey authority.[17]

The second problem with the idea of civil science (at least as we have interpreted it in recent decades) is that the universal generalizations it was supposed to produce have not panned out. The ability to predict the outcome of political and administrative dynamics is weak at best, as is the ability to come up with research findings that will guide administrators unerringly to the most effective managerial strategy. This shortcoming, by the way, seems to bother researchers much more than it does public servants. People who work in government seem to be at ease with the scarcity of firm social science results to guide decision making. They are also more skeptical about advice that is offered up as such. No doubt this is because if practical experience teaches us anything, it's that one situation is both like *and* unlike all the others in fundamental ways.[18] The sources of diversity are many, but surely one of the deepest is politics. Administrative expertise boils down to being able to tell the difference between the aspects of situations that lend themselves to the judicious application of rules (whether from science or from law and regulation) and those that don't seem to fit any rule and have to be figured out on the spot, so to speak—no small thing, by the way.

In short, Hobbes and his civil science teach us that if we want security and a sure way of achieving results, we can only have them at the cost of our freedom, at least any freedom that extends beyond the bounds of private life. Hobbes's definition of freedom is simply not being hindered from doing those things that a person has the "strength and wit" as well as the will to do in his or her own bailiwick. The purpose of the state is to create the conditions for the exercise of this sort of private freedom, not for the public freedom that is participation in politics. "Diversity of belief and interest *is* politics, but . . . this politics *is* war, and that is why diversity must be confined to the sphere of private life."[19] The more security, the less freedom. It's a zero-sum game. The influence of this way of thinking is widespread and deep.

Its persistence in American public life is strange. Hobbes's fear had concrete roots: He lived through the English Civil War, which featured the deposing and execution of the monarch. In his lifetime, the war of all against all was not just an idea. Granted the United States emerged out of a similar revolutionary impulse. But the American Revolution had a positive outcome. Strange, then, that we are so captivated by Hobbesian visions, in which political destabilization ends inevitably in disaster. Need we be? Is there another way of thinking about the relationship between security and freedom?

ANOTHER VOICE

Most, if not all, of what is being said and written about homeland security fits the vision of a dangerous world, protection from which requires people to obey the orders of the sovereign (the law) and confine their interests and opinions to the private sphere of market and family. One of the clearest alternatives to this way of thinking comes from Hannah Arendt.

Since ancient times, she observes, government has been defined as "the rule of man over man"—rule based on "the means of legitimate, that is, allegedly legitimate, violence."[20] Writers in this tradition have taken their cue from Hobbes's comment that "Covenants, without the sword, are but words."[21] The state's power is grounded in its license to exercise violence and create the conditions for the achievement of private desires.

There is "another tradition and another vocabulary no less old and time-honored," however.[22] The Athenian city-state and ancient Rome had concepts of public power not grounded in command-and-obey. In the case of the Greeks it was the idea of isonomy, or no rule; in the case of the Romans it was the idea of a republic, or the rule of law to which the citizenry had given its consent. According to Arendt, it was to these sources—especially to Rome—that the American founders looked for inspiration when they conceived of the new government.

The extent to which the framers of the U.S. Constitution were guided by this alternative tradition is debatable. In the *Federalist Papers*, for example, there is as much skepticism about human nature as faith in the people's wisdom. But Arendt is persuasive on the existence of an alternative model of government from the very earliest days on the new continent. A compact was drawn up on board the *Mayflower* as it drew near the new world. This compact reflected the Pilgrims' fear of the wilderness and the state of nature to which they were journeying. Just as palpable and even more remarkable was that "their obvious fear of one another was accompanied by the no less obvious confidence they had in their own power, granted and confirmed by no one and as yet unsupported by any means of violence, to combine themselves together into a 'civil body Politick' which, held together solely by the strength of mutual promise 'in the presence of God and one another,' supposedly was powerful enough to 'enact, constitute, and frame' all necessary laws and instruments of government."[23]

At the beginning of what became the United States was faith on the part of settlers in their common ability to craft a viable society and willingness to promise one another to do together what was required to achieve as much security and stability as possible. Arendt argues that there are significant differences between this mode of social contract, based on reciprocity and equality, and the better known type drawn up out of mutual fear.

First, although the social contract envisioned by Hobbes was an agreement among men, the agreement required each of them to transfer his own power to the state. It was a "surrender of rights and power to either the government or the community" in return for security— for protection of life and property. The contract was *I'll consent to be ruled if you will*.[24] In contrast, the Mayflower Compact and other agreements reached among the colonists in the earliest days took the form of a mutual binding together in order to constitute a community. As the compact declared, "We . . . covenant and combine ourselves together into a civill body so just and equall laws, ordinances, acts, constitutions, & offices, from time to time, as shall be thought most meete & convenient for ye generall good of ye Colonie, unto which we promise all due submission and obedience."[25]

This process presupposes the political equality of all those who join in promising, and the outcome is a society in the old Roman sense of the word, that is, an alliance. In promising, each individual gains power as he or she joins with others; in the social contract, each loses power to a government that monopolizes it. In the first, each person overcomes his or her isolation; in the second, the point of the contract is to ensure the continuance of that isolation.

Equally important, the social contract was a "fictitious, aboriginal act" whereas the agreements among the early settlers actually took place. The Mayflower Compact was signed not by "The People" but by actual human beings. We are confronted, Arendt says, with "an event rather than a theory or a tradition." Thus by the time of the American Revolution, "experience had taught the colonists that royal and company charters confirmed and legalized rather than established and founded their commonwealth."[26] The Mayflower Compact and similar agreements were constitutions in the sense that they were founding acts, not abstractions.

To be sure, a near mutiny on the part of the indentured servants and lower-class freemen on board the *Mayflower* prompted the leaders to draft their compact, which was modeled on the religious covenant.[27] Nevertheless it was a ground-breaking agreement in every sense. The signers believed that mutual promising was enough to create their government. Their act embodies the republican principle that power resides in the people, "If the people be governors, who shall be governed?"[28]

Arendt argues that the Pilgrims acted on assumptions of equal standing and equal worth that lay behind mutual promising and the common bonds that would be forged from joining together to act in freedom. Within the social contract, freedom means liberty from confining strictures that keep each man from seeking his own private happiness. For Arendt, "political freedom, generally speaking, means the right 'to be a participator in government,' or it means nothing."[29]

The Mayflower Compact became the model for other agreements, including the Cambridge Agreement drafted by members of the Massachusetts Bay Company before embarking to America in 1629. By the time of the American Revolution, mutual promising as reflected in the compact had become a well-established political precedent. These events had taught the Founding Fathers the elemental truth that power comes from the people. For them this was not a "fiction" but a "working reality."[30]

John Adams gestured toward the compact rhetorically in the years immediately preceding the Revolution. Adams said that New England's founders had known "that government was a plain, simple, intelligible thing, founded in nature and reason, and quite comprehensible by common sense."[31] Thomas Hutchinson's *History of Massachusetts*, published in 1764, declared that those who had migrated there in the early 1600s "thought themselves at full liberty, without any charter from the crown, to establish such sort of government as they thought proper, and to form a new state as full to all intents and purposes as if they had been in a state of nature, and were making their first entrance into civil society."[32] No surprise, then, that the time of the Declaration of Independence was a time of spontaneous constitution making in all the thirteen colonies, by men who saw themselves as representatives who had received their authority from the people. This grant of authority was a far different phenomenon from the conventional idea of "consent." Yet the idea of representation introduced a fatal element.

As Arendt notes, the system devised by the framers of the Constitution opened a gap between the new government and the model offered by the Mayflower Compact and similar early agreements. In adopting a representative system, they closed off to ordinary people the direct experience of political life they themselves had enjoyed. The early colonists were participators in governing in a way that is almost lost to us: They were directly involved, we are onlookers. Today the link between ordinary citizens and their representatives is stretched so thin it has almost disappeared.

The model of security inherent in the Mayflower Compact does not depend on first responders, armies, arsenals, impermeable borders, and state surveillance of daily life. No doubt some such measures may be necessary when a nation faces imminent threat. I suggest, though, that current homeland security measures remind people constantly of how insecure they really are, instead of strengthening the framework of society so people have firmer ground on which to stand. In a recent discussion about whether security can be designed, one artist criticized the current emphasis on surveillance, as in "If you see something, say something." He said, "I feel like the next [step] should be . . . 'Trust.' Security isn't locks on doors; you can put a lot of these on. But it's better to talk to your neighbor eventually."[33]

The basic point is that we must find some way of strengthening the bonds between us, even within the confines of a government system that offers few chances for public dialogue. It can only be done by means of countless small interactions in daily life over long periods of time, interactions that build the sense that we are all in this together. Otherwise we have no other source of security than the ones promised us by the state, which often turn out to be illusory anyway. Future attacks and future natural disasters are guaranteed to occur. Being lulled by government half-measures, continuing to travel and shop as usual, will not prepare us to meet the challenge.

The next two chapters will dig deeper into the neglected resources (neglected by theorists and analysts, that is) that lie within the relationships among members of a society. But perhaps a few examples would be helpful at this point. A striking aspect of the Katrina story is the number instances of which the existing social fabric not only held together but made possible mutual aid among people struggling to survive. Many persons and groups took action to help without being called out by officials; in fact, in too many cases, officials got in the way, waving red tape and rule books.

- As the floodwaters rose, a flotilla of some three hundred small craft began massing on the edges of the flooded area, heading in search of survivors. "In a culture built on fishing and intimately familiar with hurricanes, no one needed to say a word. There was a sense of duty in responding to a flood."[34]
- Members of the Florida Airboat Association contacted FEMA (the Federal Emergency Management Agency) trying to find out where they should deploy. Volunteers were told they should stay out of the disaster zone because it was not safe.[35]
- A volunteer group of paramedics who came from out of town were turned away by FEMA because they didn't have a requisition number. Undeterred, they holed up in the house of someone they knew and began collecting bodies, giving out medicine, cooking and delivering meals, and finding gas for emergency generators.[36]
- An activist named Mike Rahim, living in an unflooded area of New Orleans, sent an email to a network of activists that brought volunteers from all over the United States, hauling in food and medical supplies. The activists gathered in an abandoned mosque, spray

painted "First Aid" on an exterior wall, and gave themselves the name
Common Ground. Six days after the clinic opened, forty out-of-
state volunteers were camped around Rahim's home. By the end of
the year, 170 had rotated in and out of service at the clinic.[37]

These stories are offered as evidence of the resilience of the social
fabric during a disaster, not as evidence that government efforts are
unnecessary. They focus attention on the fact that people in a community—a neighborhood, a town, a city, a state, a nation—are all in it
together in a fundamental way and are aware of it more often than not.
Yet people displaced by Hurricane Katrina have languished for months
on end, waiting for the only community effort capable of marshaling
the resources necessary to help them rebuild after a disaster of such
magnitude: government.

John Dewey once called democracy "a mode of associated living."[38]
His observation calls attention to the importance of considering what
the dynamics of association are or could be. Americans are too apt to
see society as made up of individuals who have to fend for themselves
unless the country is under attack—sometimes even then. There is
more to democracy than voting.

Both Arendt and Thomas Hobbes experienced dark times—times
when even the most fundamental foundations of society and the state
were shaken, even collapsed. One argued that the only safety lay in plac-
ing the reins of power and knowledge in the hands of unshakeable
authority. The other suggested that the only hope of stability lies in
rekindling the light of the public world, where each of us says to one
another what we deem to be the truth.

Thus we have two visions of governance, one focused on authority,
the other on freedom. People in public service are fairly well acquainted
in today's dark times with governance rooted in the authority of the
state and the authority of science. Neither seems able to keep up with
the deepening darkness. Might we not turn toward the possibility to
which Arendt draws our attention? I mean the possibility that public
authority has its roots in people, not in the *concept* of a people who have
tacitly if not fictively turned over their authority to the state, but *real*
people in all their plurality. As Arendt said, "Not man but men inhabit

the world."[39] In the potential of plural human beings to understand, judge, promise one another, and make a world between them, lies a source of light that, though it may not be enough to vanquish the darkness, we have yet to give a fair try.

NOTES

1. Donald F. Kettl, *System under Stress: Homeland Security and American Politics* (Washington: CQ Press, 2004), 28.

2. James March and Johan Olsen, "Organizing Political Life: What Administrative Reorganization Tells Us about Government," *American Political Science Review* 77 (1983), 288, 290.

3. John R. Brinkerhoff, "Reorganizing Is Not the Solution for Homeland Security," www.homelanddefense.org/journal/articles/BrinkerhoffReorg.html. Downloaded April 14, 2003.

4. Dwight Ink, "An Analysis of the House Select Committee and White House Reports on Hurricane Katrina," *Public Administration Review* 66 (2006), 806.

5. Nate Schweber and Sean D. Hamill, "Review Set in Pennsylvania after 50-Mile Traffic Tie-Up," *New York Times*, February 17, 2007, A10.

6. David Brooks, "The Bursting Point," *New York Times*, Week in Review, September 4, 2005, 11.

7. Paul Krugman, "Killed by Contempt," *New York Times*, September 5, 2005, A23.

8. Thomas Hobbes, *Leviathan*, ed. C. B. MacPherson (Harmondsworth, UK: Penguin, 1968), sec. XIII, 186.

9. Mark Roelofs, *The Poverty of American Politics: A Theoretical Interpretation*, 2nd ed. (Philadelphia: Temple University Press, 1998), 48.

10. Donald Hanson, "Thomas Hobbes's 'Highway to Peace,'" *International Organization* 38 (1984), 329.

11. Jean Bethke Elshtain, "Reflections on War and Political Discourse," *Political Theory* 13 (1985), 40.

12. Jed Horne, *Breach of Faith: Hurricane Katrina and the Near Death of a Great American City* (New York: Random House, 2006), 108.

13. Hobbes, *Leviathan*, sec. XI, 161.

14. Ibid., 169–70.

15. Jan H. Blits, "Hobbesian Fear," *Political Theory* 17 (1989), 425.

16. Peter J. Ahrensdorf, "The Fear of Death and the Longing for Immortality: Hobbes and Thucydides on Human Nature and the Problem of Anarchy," *American Political Science Review* 94 (2000), 583; emphasis added.

17. Hobbes, *Leviathan*, sec. XXX, 379–80.

18. See Ralph P. Hummel, "Stories Managers Tell: Why They Are as Valid as Science," *Public Administration Review* 51 (1991), 31–41.

19. Hanson, "Thomas Hobbes's 'Highway to Peace,'" 353.

20. Hannah Arendt, "On Violence," in Hannah Arendt, *Crises of the Republic* (San Diego: Harcourt Brace & Co., 1972), 138.

21. Hobbes, *Leviathan*, XVII, 223.

22. Arendt, "On Violence," 139.

23. Hannah Arendt, *On Revolution* (Harmondsworth, UK: Penguin, 1977), 167. Originally published 1963.

24. Arendt, *On Revolution*, 169.

25. George F. Willison, *Saints and Strangers: Being the Lives of the Pilgrim Fathers & Their Families, with Their Friends & Foes* (Orleans, MA: Parnassus Imprints, 1945), 143.

26. Arendt, *On Revolution*, 170, 171.

27. Willison, *Saints and Strangers*, 138–46.

28. Arendt, *On Revolution*, 171. Arendt notes that the words are those of John Cotton, Puritan minister and the "Patriarch of New England" in the first half of the seventeenth century.

29. Arendt, *On Revolution*, 218.

30. Ibid., 166.

31. Wesley Frank Craven, *The Legends of the Founding Fathers* (Ithaca, NY: Cornell University Press, 1965), 29. Originally published 1956.

32. Craven, 41.

33. "Can Design Prepare for Disaster?" *New York Times*, Home and Garden section, September 9, 2005, D1, D10.

34. Horne, *Breach of Faith*, 89.

35. Ibid.

36. Christopher Cooper and Robert Block, *Disaster: Hurricane Katrina and the Failure of Homeland Security* (New York, Henry Holt, 2006), 257.

37. Horne, *Breach of Faith*, 221ff. During the Pennsylvania snowstorm mentioned above, local residents on snowmobiles and four-wheelers trekked out to the highways with food and water, while state emergency management officials failed to mention in a conference call with the governor that hundreds of people were stranded in their cars. See note 5.

38. John Dewey, *Democracy and Education* (New York: Free Press, 1916), 87.

39. Hannah Arendt, *Men in Dark Times* (San Diego: Harcourt Brace & Co., 1968), viii.

CHAPTER 5

The Social Reality of Public Space

U P TO THIS POINT WE HAVE CONSIDERED BIG QUESTIONS for administrators to think about, such as what is reason, what is truth—indeed, what thinking is itself. Now it is time to knock the pins out from under the implicit individualism of this focus and suggest that finding meaning in public life involves thinking (and acting) with others. Especially in dark times, it entails seeing reality in a way that most of us don't: as inherently social, rather than individual. I believe that no amount of self-reflection will make public life meaningful unless the individualism with which it is ordinarily understood is tempered by a framework in which its social dimension is taken into account.

This discussion is necessary because the Hobbesian view of social reality, described in the last chapter, is so well fixed in people's minds that it is hard to challenge, much less dislodge. Countless discussions with practitioners cause me to suspect that many readers are skeptical of an alternative, as suggested by the model of the Mayflower Compact, that starts from an assumption other than violent human nature.

This chapter offers an understanding of social reality as composed not of competitive, isolated individuals but of countless beings linked together in various ways. The argument begins with Rene Descartes, the other philosopher from whom we inherited our taken-for-granted view of reality.

DESCARTES AND THE SELF

Descartes formulated the theory of knowledge and reality that is implied but not spelled out in Hobbes's social and political philosophy. The latter assumed that although people's passions might keep them from seeing clearly, they were capable of understanding the nature of social reality and the need for the state by examining their own life experience. If you want to understand other people, "Read thy self." In other words, look at your own thoughts, opinions, hopes, fears, and you will know those of others.[1]

Descartes also started with looking inward, but he refused to take personal experience for granted. It was not just passions that could potentially keep people from grasping reality; it was the nature of experience itself. Descartes calls on us to treat experience itself as an object, "In objectifying the experience, I no longer accept it as what sets my norm for what it is to have knowledge."[2] In other words, experience cannot speak to us about reality directly. How do we know it is telling us the truth? I can't take my experience at face value, because I may be wrong. The refusal to trust the truth of experience opens up a huge gulf between the thinking subject and everything else—between the "in here" and the "out there."[3]

People who know nothing else about Descartes often know that he said, "I think, therefore I am." This statement reflected his beginning point of doubting the reality of everything. The one thing I can be sure of is that I think; and reason says I must exist because otherwise who is thinking this thought? He asked whether any of the ideas "in here" (inside me) actually match anything that exists "outside of me" and concluded that we can never know this as certainly as we can know our own interior stream of thoughts and ideas.

From this argument we have inherited the notions that each of us is completely separated from the world, including other people, and that knowledge of that world requires *maintaining* the posture of detachment. In order to know, we have to stop living within experience and treat it as an object. This gives us a picture of the human being as necessarily separated from the world and from other people. This view of reality and the nature of knowledge produced a "new political atomism" in the seventeenth century (Descartes and Hobbes were contemporaries). Contract theory changed as a result. In earlier versions, the prior existence of a community among human beings was taken for granted and the agreement that formed the contract took place within the enabling fabric of the community. After Descartes and Hobbes, the question became, How does the community get started?[4] There is no community until somehow people get together and consciously form it.

This question comes up only because it has already been assumed that people are basically isolated from each other, not to mention competitive and mutually threatening. The formation of a community requires somehow leaping across or bridging the gulf that separates individuals. Most of the questions raised by political philosophy since the seventeenth century address variants of the same quandary, If we are so separated and so self-interested, how is it that society and the state are possible? Most of the answers remain somewhat if not entirely unconvincing, because of the form of the question itself. The problem is framed as crafting a society and a state out of separate selves. But is there another way of thinking about human nature and reality that does not start in this way?

Heidegger's Ontology

In freeing our thinking from the trap of individualism, we must go to bedrock. From birth we experience ourselves as already in a field that contains both other beings and objects. As children we begin to sort out self and other, to differentiate ourselves from what surrounds us. In adult experience, too, at any given moment people are always already involved with things and other people.

The foremost drafter of a map to non-Cartesian reality is philosopher Martin Heidegger. He rejected the idea of the isolated ego doubting the reality of the world, arguing that doubt itself puts being here before thinking: Cartesian reasoning reveals an already in-the-world doubter.[5] He called it a "scandal of philosophy" to be obsessed with the lack of proof for the existence of the external world. We go on believing that we need such proofs, and philosophers keep providing them.[6] Yet "from birth on, we experience ourselves as a being that is in the company of others."[7] This view of reality starts not with a lonely person somewhere in nonspace (virtual space?) but with beings-in-the-world with other beings. In fact, even to talk of "beings" in relation to a "world" is misleading. Heidegger argues rather that *Dasein* (i.e., "being here"—the term he used in order to avoid talking about individuals or subjects) is "in-itself essentially Being-with."[8]

To grasp the importance and plausibility of this way of looking at reality, one only has to realize that there is no more (and no less) evidence for this way than for the other. Both are equally possible—or equally impossible. So how do we choose between them?

Until now, the choice has been made for you. You inherited it. You grew up seeing the world and other people as out there and yourself as in here. You inherited the idea that the biggest issue in acquiring knowledge of the world out there was to figure out how to bridge the gap between your ideas of the world and the way it "really is." But there is no more evidence that people are essentially isolated than that they are essentially connected. Ontology (a theory about reality, a theory about being) is something you start with, not something you prove. To ask a pragmatic question, From the point of view of someone in public service, which view of reality helps us to find meaning in public life?

Of course, different people have different understandings of the meaning they are searching for. But the view of governance most prevalent now—the one grounded in market theories and objectified views of state and society—separates people to such an extent, and relies so much on ideas of self-interest and competition, that the whole idea of shared public life is becoming shadowy and insubstantial. Certain writers on governance have advanced the metaphor of the "hollow state" to capture this thinning out of the idea of the public. But it is not just the state that has become hollow; citizens' and public servants' experience of public life and politics is hollow too. We don't feel connected to other people. The idea of connection seems like a dream. There are quite straightforward, nonphilosophical reasons for why we feel this way, such as politicians'"camouflage and double-talk," of which Hannah Arendt spoke in *Men in Dark Times*. But in order to see our way toward another form of public life, we have to start at bedrock and *assume* that we are all already connected, just as we have assumed in the past that we were

not. This is the first step toward seeing ourselves as part of a community, rather than part of a great cloud of unconnected dots.

The rest of this chapter fleshes out how we know and connect with
one another and lays the groundwork for a theory of governance in the
next chapter.

The Social Construction of Reality

Sociological theories of intersubjectivity, particularly the work of Alfred
Schutz, explore what people know in a taken-for-granted way about
everyday reality. This knowledge makes up "the fabric of meanings
without which no society could exist."[9] In other words, each of us does
not encounter the world anew and make sense of it alone. Quite the
contrary. We are born into an already existing social world made up
of shared understandings about the meaning of things and events and
shared skills about how to go on in daily life. These understandings and
skills are almost entirely taken for granted and indeed operate below the
level of awareness unless something unusual comes along to stop the
flow of shared experience.

Schutz argued that each of us makes two assumptions that are the
foundation of the common world. First, I take for granted that if I
change places with somebody else so that his or her "here" becomes
mine, I will see things just the way the other person did, at least for all
practical purposes. For example, if I step into a job someone has just
left, by and large I will see the organization and the roles of its people
pretty much the same way as the person I replaced. I will take for
granted, as that person did, that the organization has a head, that there
is a chain of command, that at the end of two weeks I will get a pay-
check, that if the copying machine breaks down there is a specific person to ask for help, and so on. True, entering a new organization does
require a period of learning the ropes, of getting the hang of "how we
do things here," but this period will not be like landing on another
planet. I will already share a great many understandings that I won't have
to develop for myself.

The second assumption is that even though the person I replaced has
had different life experiences from mine—she grew up in the South, I

in the North; she was an only child, I have several brothers and sisters—
these differences will be largely irrelevant for the purposes at hand,
that is, for doing the job and fitting into the organization. Schutz
argues that these two assumptions, which all human beings make about
social reality, in fact establish and maintain it. They are the foundation
of a common world "which transcends the actors' private experiential
worlds."[10] This common world has been constructed by the human
beings who share it; day by day, they go on constructing it.

Schutz's notion of intersubjective reality is not a solution to the
problem of how people manage to inhabit the same society without
killing each other (at least most of the time). In the social world, both
cooperation and conflict occur. But "at the end of the day, conflict, just
as much as cooperation, can only be conducted within an overarching
framework of intelligibility."[11] In other words, the very notion of conflict has a widely shared meaning that is the product of social interaction, preeminently of language use. We could not worry about conflict
if we didn't agree, by and large, about what the term meant. And this
agreement is evidence of a pre-given, socially constructed reality.

Recall that the idea of someone who doubts the existence of the
world *presupposes* that the doubter already finds him- or herself in the
very world he or she has called into question. The idea of intersubjectivity builds on this premise. It calls on us to stop taking for granted
the picture of the world we have inherited and offers a deeper perspective on the social world.

The theory of the social construction of reality can account for
why changing our way of looking at social reality is not easy. I depend
on my ongoing sense of everyday life to go on in it. Everyday reality is
ordered—it makes sense to me—and it presents itself to me as a world
I share with others. In fact I can't exist in this everyday world without
interacting and communicating with other people.[12] Our dependence
on the social world is so deeply rooted that it has been argued that
without it we would not be human at all, because we would not have
the shared network of understandings, including a shared language,
that are, at the most fundamental level, what make us human. "One is
a self only among other selves."[13] The Tarzan story tells us that when
the baby raised in the wild by apes is brought into human society, he

cannot function. He has no language and it is too late for him to learn one. Therefore he cannot join the web of shared understandings. In the eyes of society, he is not human.

Little wonder, then, that many people find it hard to question assumptions about human nature and society that are as pervasive as the ones we inherited from Descartes and Hobbes. These perspectives long ago left the rarified world of philosophy and became part of the fabric of taken-for-granted reality.

The sociologist Harold Garfinkel spent his life experimenting to expose this fabric—the ongoing work people do to construct and maintain social situations. He believes that shared understandings are not just a form of knowledge. They also have a moral dimension: if someone in a situation does something that doesn't fit, he or she will be asked to account for the anomaly. Others in a situation perceive incongruent actions not only as out of sync but as morally wrong, unless the actor can give an account of his or her actions that is consistent with shared rules of behavior. Typically, these rules are not articulated until, in the eyes of others, something does go wrong.

Numerous experiments, many of them with the help of students, brought to light the force with which shared assumptions structure ordinary situations. In one experiment, students were told to engage with a friend in a conversation but to question very ordinary or routine statements. For example: Someone says to the student-experimenter, "I had a flat tire." The student-experimenter answers, "What do you mean, you had a flat tire?" The first speaker appears momentarily stunned. Then she replies in an irritated way, "What do you mean, 'What do you mean?' A flat tire is a flat tire. That is what I mean. Nothing special. What a crazy question!" The student who had the flat tire takes it for granted that everyone knows what a flat tire is. She doesn't have to explain it. When the student-experimenter asks for an explanation, her reaction is negative, What is wrong with you? Everybody knows what a flat tire is! Get a grip![14]

A simple test like this one throws the ongoing fabric of shared assumptions into bold relief by stopping the flow. It reveals how thoroughly woven together human beings are by means of an uncountable number of common meanings and understandings. This work also shows how conversations between people rely on unspoken assumptions. We all mean much more than we can say. Not only do we take for granted that we don't have to lay out every detail of the substance of what we want to communicate, we assume people already know a lot of what we want to tell them, including the definitions of the words we use.

There is also quite a bit communicated that we *can't* say. Take the example of trying to teach someone else to knit. How much of it can you say in words? Quite a bit, but suppose that you didn't have yarn and needles handy and you couldn't illustrate with hand gestures. (Maybe the two of you are talking on the phone.) Do you think you could explain it well enough so the other person could actually learn to knit just by what you said? Or, to put it another way, do you think that everything you know about knitting can be put into words? (Those who don't knit can substitute throwing a baseball, fixing a faucet, or playing a musical instrument.) Yet somehow people pass on knowledge that can't be spoken aloud. Could we do this, as we routinely do, unless we were already connected to one another?

At this point, sociology links itself to Heidegger's views on the nature of reality. As Ralph Hummel explains, "We already understand each other before language comes along." Speech does not create the possibility of mutual understanding, "Rather, it is because we already fundamentally understand each other to be fellow human beings that speech is possible."[15] Could we construct reality, as these sociologists have argued we do, if this fundamental understanding did not underlie our life with others?

The idea that reality is socially constructed calls attention to the existence of community not as a thing, like a building or a machine, but as a *process*. Buried within the forms of knowledge and the views of the state we inherited from Descartes and Hobbes (among others) is the assumption that societies, communities, and other social phenomena are objects somehow disconnected, or at least distinguishable, from the people who comprise them. A famous sociologist in this tradition once said, "Consider social facts as things."[16] But what if we consider them as processes rather than objects?

Mary Parker Follett, one of the most creative writers on organizations, suggested we do this. In the early twentieth century, Follett proposed a view of reality that gave equal weight to the individual and the social. She saw individual selves not as fixed but as constantly being formed and re-formed from their immersion in social interactions. Individuals are individuals, she argued, but what sustains them is relation, "the ceaseless interplay of the One and the Many by which both are constantly making each other."[17] The fact that the individual and the social are interwoven, said Follett, makes ideas of political representation or the division of power completely off the mark. To see governments and organizations formed around declared purposes is a mistake. Community process *creates* common purpose and is constantly evolving it. (More about a process understanding of governance in the next chapter.)

PUBLIC LIFE

How do we bring this philosophy and this sociology into our understanding of public life? Perhaps the first step is to remind ourselves of the view of politics we have taken so thoroughly for granted. It is easy to find supporting evidence by just watching TV or reading the newspaper—politics built on the assumption that human beings are *by nature* separated, isolated, competitive, and violent. Ordinary politics leaps from this assumption to the conclusion that the only way to live together is to construct a system of external controls that rely on individual blame and punishment. We turn our freedom over to Leviathan—to a government in which the vast majority of us have no say over what happens, other than pulling a lever or touching a screen in the voting booth. We turn the power over to our leaders and tell them to keep us all in line and punish anyone who transgresses. The state's job is to referee the competition for spoils.

As I suggested earlier, however, this view, labeled "realism" in order to tar any alternative view with the brush of fantasy, is no more real than any other way of looking at public life. We may not have made it up—we were born into it—but we are responsible for keeping it going. There is nothing objective or logically necessary about a paranoid politics based on the proposition that people are inherently violent. We *choose* to accept that premise. No doubt we are all capable of some sort of violence under certain circumstances, but this is a different notion from the one that encourages us to see violence as threatening to break out at any time, as inevitable unless steps are taken to keep it at bay.

I said earlier that on its face mutual promising appears rather insubstantial when compared to the supposedly realistic idea of the war of all against all. Actually, though, the idea of promising is grounded in an intersubjective understanding of social reality. Public life is always already there for us if we permit ourselves to see it: a web of relationships rather than a mass of unconnected (unless they are fighting) dots. On this basis we can see constructed understandings and values as the building material of a public world.

Arendt says that the term "public" has two aspects. "It means, first, that everything that appears in public can be seen and heard by everybody. . . . The presence of others who see what we see and hear what we hear assures us of the reality of the world and ourselves."[18] Publicness refers to what we experience in common, which is real to us precisely because we do share the experience. In this sense, public life is socially constructed. Second, "public" refers to the world itself, not in the usual sense of that which is external to the thinking mind, but the intersubjective reality we humans have formed among ourselves and the public affairs we enter into with one another. The world for Arendt is preeminently humanmade: "To live together in the world means essentially that a world of things is between those who have it in common, as a table is located between those who sit around it; the world, like every in-between, relates and separates men at the same time."[19]

This leads to two fundamental ways of conceiving of public life. First, the events and things of which it is made up are humanly generated. Second, this human action *both* puts individual humans in relationship to one another *and* keeps them from becoming a mob. The key factor making this delicate construction possible is human difference, human uniqueness. We come together in public space as people who share concerns and perspectives and as beings each of whom is unique. Arendt emphasizes uniqueness in order to offer a picture of the public world as a space that brings people together but does not allow them to merge into a faceless One, a mass without daylight between members.

Thus Arendt brilliantly transforms the differences that have so worried political philosophers into absolutely necessary resources for politics. There could be no public life if people did not share certain qualities and perspectives and at the same time display fundamental differences. Every point of view that wipes out these differences, such as that we are all basically violent, destroys politics, which *is* conversations and arguments among people who are different but also share common concerns. As Arendt puts it:

> the reality of the public realm relies on the simultaneous presence of innumerable perspectives and aspects in which the common world presents itself and for which no common measurement or denominator can ever be devised. For though the common world is the common meeting ground of all, those who are present have different locations in it. . . . Everybody sees and hears from a different position. . . . Only where things can be seen by many in a variety of aspects without changing their identity, so that those who are gathered around them know they see sameness in utter diversity, can worldly reality truly and reliably appear.[20]

Because of Descartes, we lost the sense of having the world in common and replaced it with the view that what we have in common is the structure of our minds—that is, the ability to reason. Paradoxically, though, we cannot have reason "in common"—that is, we can't practice it together. We share it only in the sense that each of us who calculates two plus two will come up with the same answer. Reason, then, is "a process which man at any moment can let loose within himself."[21] It contributes nothing to making and keeping a common world. It is simply "the playing of the mind with itself."[22]

The common world depends, instead, on a "common sense," or to avoid the ordinary connotation of the term, a *sensus communis*, or sense of commonality. This idea, derived from Kant, means "a sixth sense,"[23] which is our capacity to share and understand among one another our varied perceptions and interpretations of the world.

This view of the public world conceives of human beings as fundamentally linked rather than isolated. The sense of the common is the human capacity that enables us to make (literally make, through our interactions) a public world that brings us together without wiping out our differences from one another. The public world makes it possible, as discussed in chapter 3, for us to consider an issue from the standpoint of another: not in order to become that other person, but to understand how the world looks when I myself stand in a different place and therefore to exercise considered judgment.

BACK TO REALITY?

Near the end of *The Human Condition*, Arendt observes that Hobbes based his theory of the state on the operations of the individual mind. The state is held to be an utterly rational construction, just as a machine is. The need for the state, and the form it must take, can be reasoned abstractly, based solely on the introspected elements of human nature, which are assumed to be the same for everybody.

But according to Arendt the problem with this approach is that it is utterly disconnected from reality, even though Hobbes is constantly being held up as the paragon of realism in politics: "The idea that only what I am going to make will be real . . . is forever defeated by the actual course of events, where nothing happens more frequently than the totally unexpected. To act in the form of making, to reason in the form of 'reckoning with consequences,' means to leave out the unexpected, *the event itself.*"[24]

Since September 11, 2001, and the devastating hurricanes of 2005, can there be any doubt that events exceed the best efforts of humankind to plan, strategize, rationalize, predict, and control? The entire edifice of the state has been based on excluding social reality from the realm of human affairs. Continuing to cling to these received wisdoms seems the height (or the depth) of unreality. As Arendt said, human affairs are the realm where "the wholly improbable happens regularly." It is completely unrealistic "not to reckon with something with which nobody can safely reckon. . . . [Reality] and human reason have parted company."[25]

Violent and isolated human beings are a dead end as the foundation for public life. Can we reject false realism in favor of a kind of realism that makes it possible for us to come to terms with "the eventfulness of the event"? Can we see public life as a space in which we are both differentiated and linked? There is more to governance than the supervision of who gets what, when, and how. Let us reflect on what that might be.

NOTES

1. Thomas Hobbes, *Leviathan*, ed. C. B. MacPherson (Harmondsworth, UK: Penguin, 1968), 82.

2. Charles Taylor, *The Sources of the Self: The Making of Modern Identity* (Cambridge, MA: Harvard University Press, 1989), 162.

3. Susan Bordo, "The Cartesian Masculinization of Thought," *Signs* 11 (1986), 443.

4. Taylor, 193.

5. Leslie Paul Thiele, *Timely Meditations: Martin Heidegger and Postmodern Politics* (Princeton, NJ: Princeton University Press, 1995), 46.

6. Simon Glendenning, *On Being with Others: Heidegger, Derrida, Wittgenstein* (London: Routledge, 1998), 44.

7. Ralph P. Hummel, *The Bureaucratic Experience*, 4th ed. (New York: St. Martin's Press, 1994), 179.

8. Thiele, *Timely Meditations*, 52.

9. Peter L. Berger and Thomas Luckmann, *The Social Construction of Reality* (Harmondsworth, UK: Peregrine Books, 1979), 27.

10. Alfred Schutz, "Common-Sense and Scientific Interpretation of Human Action," in Schutz, *Collected Papers, Volume I: The Problem of Social Reality*, ed. Maurice Natanson (The Hague: Martinus Nijhoff, 1967), 11–12.

11. John Heritage, *Garfinkel and Ethnomethodology* (Cambridge, UK: Polity Press, 1984), 55.

12. Berger and Luckmann, *Social Construction*, 37.

13. Taylor, *Sources of the Self*, 35.

14. Harold Garfinkel, *Studies in Ethnomethology* (Cambridge, UK: Polity Press, 1984), 42.

15. Hummel, *Bureaucratic Experience*, 179.

16. Emile Durkheim, *The Rules of Sociological Method*, 2nd ed. (New York: Free Press, 1964), 14.

17. Mary Parker Follett, "Community Is a Process," *Philosophical Review* 28 (1919), 582.

18. Hannah Arendt, *The Human Condition* (Chicago and London: University of Chicago Press, 1958), 50.

19. Ibid., 52.

20. Ibid., 57.

21. Ibid., 283.

22. Ibid., 284.

23. Jerome Kohn, "Evil and Plurality: Hannah Arendt's Way to the Life of the Mind," in *Arendt Twenty Years Later*, ed. Larry May and Jerome Kohn (Cambridge, MA: MIT Press, 1996), 171.

24. Arendt, *The Human Condition*, 300, italics added.

25. Ibid., 208.

CHAPTER 6

Governance from the Ground Up

THE MEANING OF THE TERM GOVERNANCE HAS SHIFTED.
Two decades ago, when people in public life talked about governance, it was to refer broadly to what they themselves were
doing: exercising public authority to fulfill a public purpose. The term
took in not just administrative techniques and management approaches
but also a sense of the political. Governance implied more than getting
results. It implied concern for the public good—statesmanship.

Over the last two decades, governance has acquired a new connotation. Government—the state—is no longer the defining ingredient.
Governance has expanded to include activities in the private and nonprofit sector and in fact is widely understood to mean an alternative to,
a replacement for, direct government action. The state is no longer the
star player on the field. There are so many other players, and their roles
are so diverse, that it is sometimes hard to figure out what game is being
played or what rules are being followed.

Most people don't spend a lot of time pondering changes in the
meaning of governance. Inside and outside governments, however, it is
clear that the list of activities assigned exclusively to the state has shortened dramatically. There are fewer and fewer responsibilities accepted
as "inherently governmental," to use the language of federal regulations.
Executing and monitoring contracts, diplomacy, property acquisition
and management, and financial management make the list; not much
else does.[1]

This paradigm shift has reshaped the conversation about the relationship between citizens and governments. The citizen–government connection was a big concern among those who cared about public service, when the popular image of government was a remote bureaucracy wrapped in red tape. How could ordinary folk influence such a behemoth? How could they feel a sense of connection to it? Articles and books were written about making government more accessible to citizens, expanding their authority, involving them in decision making and implementation, and improving accountability mechanisms. Sometimes the recommendations were even acted upon! Now that the State has become "hollow," as one metaphor puts it, the conversation has shifted to devolution, privatization, networks, and markets, and the question of citizens' role in government has almost disappeared. Instead the focus is on partnerships, contracts, networks, and other mechanisms that link governments with private groups for policy implementation and service delivery.

The most keenly felt effects of the new governance on public organizations are a relentless emphasis on performance, particularly in the handling of contracts, and a deepening sense that there is nothing special or even particularly worthy about public service. Government is said to be only one actor among many; the real action is elsewhere. No surprise, then, that many dedicated professionals are leaving government service and taking their skills, experience, and institutional memory with them.

From the point of view of nonprofit contractors, the biggest changes are a vastly expanded set of responsibilities and rising management performance expectations, rarely matched by greater bargaining power or political clout. The traditional role of nonprofits as advocates for their clients and as schools of democratic practice grows less and less plausible as community-based organizations struggle to become businesslike.[2]

For both public and nonprofit organizations, the role of citizens in governing has been moved to the back burner, if not off the stove entirely. The central questions in the new governance revolve around effectiveness ("results"), how to strike the most advantageous bargain with other members of the network, and accountability in the sense of ensuring that the deliverables get where they need to go and arrive on time.

A lot has been written and discussed about the transformation of citizen to customer. Critics have pointed out that the customer can decide whether or not to purchase goods in the market but has little say about what is available.[3] This model fits poorly into the public sector, where much of what is done is the result of market failure and many government services cannot be freely rejected. (Can you shop around when you need a driver's license or when your house is on fire?) In a system where the people are supposed to be not just shoppers but sovereign, even some free marketeers can see the difference between citizen and customer, though they may not think the difference matters.

In the new governance, the contest between economic thinking and citizen thinking is a very unequal one. The point is to create a supportive environment for a free market economy. So even though advocates of so-called good governance, particularly on the international level, generally call for political renewal and advocate participation, democratic elements function only as tools for the maintenance of market freedom, not as ends in themselves. A clear example is the World Bank's "good governance" development policy in Africa.[4] This and other such perspectives are built on the assumption that democratic political freedom is necessary in order to support market freedom. But these two freedoms are very different from one another. And the question of which of them is more fundamental is, ultimately, a philosophical rather than an instrumental question.

TWO FREEDOMS

Hobbes defines freedom, or "liberty," as "the absence of Opposition."[5] You are free when you are not prevented from choosing what you will do. If a man is on a ship and throws his goods over the side because he is afraid the ship is about to sink that is his free choice; he could refuse if he wanted. Because you do something out of fear doesn't mean you aren't free. Liberty is the absence of coercion.

In the same way, liberty is consistent with necessity. Dealing a blow to the age-old argument over whether human action is free (as in free will) or driven by external causes, Hobbes maintains that action can be both free and caused at the same time, "as in the water, that hath not only liberty, but a necessity of descending by the Channel."[6] There may be factors causing you to do what you do, but that doesn't mean that you aren't free.

When it comes specifically to political freedom, Hobbes declares that it lies in being able to do anything you like as long as the sovereign hasn't specifically forbidden it. If there is no law against something, you are free to do it. Liberty is privatized, "to buy, and sell, and otherwise contract with one another; to choose [one's] own aboad, . . . diet, . . . trade of life," and way of raising one's children—in other words, the sort of freedom found in the free market. But Hobbes, in referring to this as "the Liberty of a Subject," means us to understand that market freedom is the same thing as political freedom.[7] We should not worry that there are no opportunities to join in governing the state. We have turned governing over to the sovereign so that we can be safe from one another. If we are free in our private lives, including our dealings in the market, what other freedom do we need?

Hobbes does place one limit on the power of Leviathan. He asks "what are the things, which though commanded by the Soveraign, [a person] may neverthelesse, without injustice, refuse to do." Must we do whatever the sovereign commands us to do? Yes, with one exception. The sovereign does not have the right to tell a person to do himself or herself harm, "to kill, wound, or mayme himselfe; or not to resist those that assault him; or to abstain from the use of food, ayre, medicine, or any other thing, without which he cannot live."[8] The sovereign can put us to death if we break laws that carry the death penalty but not command us to kill ourselves. The right of self-preservation is bedrock. (Think, for example, about the various places in the legal system in which self-defense becomes the determining principle.) If it were not, the whole agreement on which the state is based would be pointless. The core of the philosophy of limited government lies in the statement, "As for other Lyberties, they depend on the silence of the Law."[9] Freedom is freedom from state interference other than whatever is necessary to keep us secure. Beyond that, Leviathan should keep quiet.

As I argued in the previous chapter, this position makes some sense as long as it is assumed that human reality is made up of isolated, potentially violent individuals. But the presumption of violence is not an empirical proposition that can be confirmed or disconfirmed once and for all by reality itself. It is an assumption we start with and use to make sense of experience. We have been born into it but we keep it going with our own beliefs and actions. We can choose to set it aside in favor of alternative ones that permit us to interpret events differently and envision other ways of living together. For thinking about freedom, a view of reality in which humans are primordially linked rather than isolated, leads us once again to Hannah Arendt.

In Arendt's view "political freedom, generally speaking, means the right to be a participator in government, or it means nothing."[10] No greater contrast with freedom as private liberty can be imagined. How does she get there? Certainly not by ignoring the prevailing view. Her own life had been led in the midst of war and other kinds of violence. Arendt was no Pollyanna. She wrote a devastating critique of totalitarianism, that is, of states where nothing is beyond the reach of the government. She understood not only the persuasiveness of the idea of protection from mutual violence but the value human beings place on holding some part of their lives safe from the reach of government. It is understandable that we tend to define freedom as freedom *from* politics, that is, "Do we not rightly measure the extent of freedom in any given community by the free scope it grants to apparently nonpolitical activities, free economic enterprise or freedom of teaching, of religion, of cultural and intellectual activities?"[11]

But there is more to freedom than freedom *from*. Negative liberties, freedom from want and fear, freedom from restraints on speech, worship, and so on are important, but it is a mistake to think that they exhaust the meaning of the word. To expand it, Arendt focuses on the leaders of the American Revolution. The Declaration of Independence calls for "life, liberty, and the pursuit of happiness." The happiness referred to in the Declaration was public rather than private: "Americans knew that public freedom consisted in having a share in public business, and that the activities connected with this business by no means constituted a burden. Rather they gave those who discharged them in public a feeling of happiness they could acquire nowhere else."[12] The freedom won in the Revolution was not just liberty but happiness, not just protection in order to pursue private happiness, but the public happiness that came from the citizen's right to be (in Thomas Jefferson's words) "a participator in the government of affairs."[13]

As the new U.S. government developed, however, the perceived importance of public happiness faded. Happiness was redefined as the pursuit
of private interests without government interference. Thus Americans
came to think of liberty in a negative way—as freedom from. Arendt
argues that one important reason for this development was that the governmental system established in the Constitution made very little room
for direct participation by ordinary citizens. A system of representation
was set up in which the views of average people were filtered through
a complicated network of levels of government, branches, separated
powers, and checks and balances. With rare to nonexistent opportunity
to join directly in governing, it was easy for people to perceive government as remote and unapproachable. Arendt writes, "The Revolution,
while it had given freedom to the people, had failed to provide a space
where this freedom could be exercised. Only the representatives of the
people, not the people themselves, had an opportunity to engage in those
activities of 'expressing, discussing, and deciding' which in a positive
sense are the activities of freedom."[14]

Arendt defines the political as the form of activity that establishes and
keeps in existence a space of freedom. As people talk to one another,
each from a different perspective, about issues and concerns they share,
a political space comes into existence. The way the conversation unfolds
is completely unpredictable because every human being is a new beginning, someone who has never lived before and never will again, who is
unlike anyone else. The political depends on this fundamental fact about
human beings; as Arendt puts it, "that not Man but men live upon the
earth." When human beings come together around common concerns,
their talk both unites and separates them. It unites them in the sense
that it links their differences together around a shared issue. It also separates them: They see things differently so they can't turn into a mob.[15]
"Freedom exists only in the unique intermediary space of politics,"[16]
she says. In Arendt's view, freedom is freedom to.

REDEFINING GOVERNANCE

Today's new governance is premised on a view of political freedom
as freedom from politics. What people want from the state is basic

protection from one another (e.g., protection from terrorist attacks) so they can go after whatever material possessions or social status they think will make them happy. Freedom means being able to do whatever they want short of doing violence to someone else. The state should protect them and guarantee their right to pursue their interests, but otherwise get out of the way. Political freedom is negative: freedom from interference.

Based on these premises, plus the assumption that the economic playing field is level, the new governance conceives of the activities of governing as reducing what government does in favor of farming things out to private actors (whether profit-making or nonprofit). To the extent possible, the market is to control the distribution of goods and promote competition. The connection between citizens and their governments takes a contractual form. There is nothing special about government other than its responsibility to guarantee basic physical security: to keep people from trampling over one another in the pursuit of private goods and to protect against external threats.

Advocates of new governance defend reliance on the market, but are blind to the role government plays in stabilizing it. They see contracting and deal making as preferable to the dead hand of bureaucracy. Administrative agencies are seen as tangled in red tape. An overabundance of regulations stifles innovation, increases the cost of programs, and reduces freedom—the freedom to do as you like. Instead, relations between governments and private entities are to be negotiated so that mutually acceptable agreements are reached. Market control, to the extent that it is necessary, will be achieved by means of these agreements rather than by policy decisions or regulations. Hence the emphasis in the new paradigm on seeing governance as what goes on in networks of public-private arrangements rather than in government itself.

A number of criticisms have been leveled at this vision of governance. First, there is the question of whether markets and networks can be counted on to keep the kind of order citizens expect even from the minimal state. This is a kind of "who's minding the state" criticism. What happens when all or most of the focus and energy in governance are aimed at negotiating individual contracts and shaping various networks, and no one is looking at the big picture?[17] This question grows increasingly urgent as more information becomes available about the extent of federal contracting. Contractors not only produce weapons and supplies, they also staff government meetings, do technical work on agency budgets, and even investigate fraud on the part of other contractors.[18] Contractors have even exercised state violence, as in the torture revealed at Abu Ghraib.

A second criticism has to do with accountability. "When public functions are delegated to private actors and are allowed to be transformed into 'private' actions, public accountability is inevitably lost" because transparency is lost. This is especially true when the line between public and private becomes so blurred that no one party to a particular arrangement is really sure who has ultimate authority and over what. Sometimes this ambiguity is used strategically to avoid responsibility, for example, in the savings and loan bailout of the 1980s, which was deliberately made so complicated that assigning responsibility to specific actors became impossible.[19] As long as accountability is restricted to market values such as cost, efficiency, and customer satisfaction, questions of who has the power to exercise *public* authority and whether the public interest is being served cannot be addressed. In other words, the entire governance process has been depoliticized in the sense that debates over basic democratic values have been eliminated.

Yet another criticism asks, What happens over the long term to democracy? Is it not possible that even the fragile threads that connect citizens to their governments in the more traditional forms of statecraft will not survive the privatization of public services?[20] It may be that the "hollow state" in the long run will not retain the capacity to deliver even the minimal sort of security and protection demanded by the social contract. It may lack the substantive heft to win and keep the confidence and trust of citizens necessary to societal stability and order. Citizens may want more from their governments than efficient execution and management of contracts. They may want a sense of attachment to it. Peace cannot only be imposed from the top; it has to be woven from below. A model of governance that neglects democratic politics and the cultivation of civic engagement may fail even on its own terms.

What this means is that an alternative is worth imagining—not a return to the previous version, which defined governance as statecraft on the part of government administrators, but a model built on assumptions that a shared reality already exists, one that envisions the state as the outgrowth of mutual promising, and politics as talk that brings different people together around mutual concerns.[21]

GOVERNANCE ACCORDING TO ARENDT AND FOLLETT

A frequent criticism of any form of governance based on active citizens is that it's a nice idea but it won't work. So perhaps it might be worth stating a few real-life examples as evidence that it will.

The first example comes from Arendt herself. *On Revolution* discusses an almost forgotten pattern of events. After several revolutions in the nineteenth and twentieth centuries, community-based councils of ordinary people sprang spontaneously into being before any formal government had been established. These councils aspired to bring order into the space cleared by the revolutionary process, and they took as their watchword "the direct participation of every citizen in the public affairs of the country." Arendt observes that "every individual found his own sphere of action and could behold, as it were, with his own eyes his own contribution to the events of the day."[22]

The same thing happened after the Hungarian Revolution of 1956, when neighborhood councils emerged over the course of only a few days—councils that began to coordinate and organize with one another, fashioning a process that was intended to result in the selection of delegates to a national assembly. "We see here how the federal principle, the principle of league and alliance among separate units, arises out of the elementary conditions of action itself, uninfluenced by any theoretical speculations about the possibilities of republican government in large territories" (a reference to James Madison's theory in *Federalist Paper* #10) "and not even threatened into coherence by a common enemy."[23] So much for fear as the prime political motivator!

The emergence of neighborhood councils in so many countries under similar conditions contradicts the view of human beings as lawless and violent, unless constrained by Leviathan. And indeed the vision of people emerging from their houses as soon as the bombs stop exploding to begin constructing their own order is a poor fit with much of the political thinking we take for granted—the need for order imposed from the top, for example. In contrast to Madison's argument that the views of ordinary people had to be filtered through a representative system to refine and cool them, Arendt offers the idea of freedom as the opportunity to be a participator.[24]

The second example is today's federally supported community health center program. Over one thousand centers at five thousand sites in poor urban neighborhoods and rural areas are governed by community people serving as board members. Federal law, relatively unchanged since the days of the war on poverty, requires board members to make substantive decisions about services, personnel, fees for services, and other aspects of running the centers. I researched these centers two decades ago after working in several of them and serving as a board member for one. They exemplified what I call active citizenship. Citizens made crucial policy decisions for their centers and did so out of concern for furthering the wider interests of their communities rather than their own selfish interests. Today federal support for the centers still comes in the form of grants rather than contracts. This means that the citizens of the centers, instead of checking off a mechanical set of deliverables listed in a contract, exercise the kind of discretionary public authority over center policy that public administrators themselves do at the next level up. The grant program also makes it necessary for citizens to work collaboratively with federal officials, instead of just having their actions "monitored."[25] Citizens of the health centers are participators. They experience the kind of freedom that only comes from having a share in governance.

The third example focuses on the establishment by charter amendment of neighborhood councils in Los Angeles in 1999. Wisely the enabling amendment left it up to the people themselves to define neighborhood boundaries. The system, supported by a newly created Department of Neighborhood Empowerment, serves as a mechanism for connecting citizens with city government around service delivery in identifying existing problems, designing improved processes, and putting together a work plan targeted at a specific problem. This is a less radical departure from governing as usual than the spontaneous emergence of postrevolutionary councils but potentially more stable and long lasting.[26]

The network of councils established in Los Angeles differs significantly from the way networks are ordinarily understood in the literature of the new (market-based) governance. Members of market-based networks are organizations. Network theory sees them as primary actors (businesses, nonprofit organizations) collaborating among themselves and with government for the purpose of service delivery. The rationale of the collaborative network is understood to be maximizing program effectiveness, though it has been pointed out that beneath the rhetorical veneer of results sometimes lies a government interest in distancing the state itself from responsibility for solving messy, insoluble problems (for example, AIDS in the 1980s).[27]

In contrast, the Los Angeles network of councils is fundamentally political. Although the discussions among council members and city representatives center around solving service delivery problems, all parties understand that the origin of the system was political (triggered by the threat of several geographic areas to secede from the city), and involvement of citizens in working on problems is at least as important as solving the problems, if not more. Neighborhood councils are not organizations in the sense that businesses and nonprofit agencies are. They are alliances of neighbors. In these respects, the Los Angeles network of neighborhood councils counts as an example of the practice of political freedom. The point has been to create public space, which has democratic value in and of itself regardless of the extent to which problems get solved and services get delivered.[28]

Mary Parker Follett, one of the earliest writers in public administration, had a similar vision of what she called the "new state." Writing in 1918, she argued that "neighborhood consciousness" could be developed by regular meetings to consider neighborhood problems, by genuine discussion, by learning together, by taking more responsibility for the neighborhood, and by maintaining a formal connection to city, state, and national governments. Her vision of neighborhood government was based on her years of involvement in what was known as the community centers movement, which started as a push to get schools to remain open at night for community activities. Community centers soon became the centers of gravity for a host of educational and civic efforts, including classes of various kinds, clubs, and government meetings.

Follett argued that community centers created a "communal bond" that was expressed in "communal action." Slowly, she said, "neighborhood consciousness" will build up, so that people come to understand themselves as part of something valuable that has meaning beyond themselves.[29]

Follett contrasted this sort of group discussion with political party meetings. She thought that parties produced a crowd because the point was to get everybody to think alike. In the neighborhood meeting, in contrast, "an infinitely varied number of points of view can be brought out, and thus the final decision will be richer from what it gains on all sides."[30]

Not content simply with democracy on the neighborhood level, Follett thought out a model of the state from the ground up, so to speak, with neighborhood councils as the foundation of an entire system of government. She argued that members of the councils should meet with each other and "correlate" their needs so they were added up and transmitted to city governments and thence to the state and national levels. Councils would send representatives to city councils and state legislatures and would also be required to send in reports of neighborhood activities.[31]

The flow could also be in the other direction, as happened during World War I. A Council of National Defense was linked to State Councils, which in turn were linked to County Councils and often from there to councils in cities and towns. Plans were being made to extend this system to the neighborhood level. The entire system was seen as necessary to keep the nation safe. What a contrast with current homeland security measures!

Follett saw a *natural* tendency of genuine groups (that is, groups where people expressed different opinions to one another as they worked to solve common problems) to come together and form collaborations. (Note the difference from the network of hierarchical organizations.) "Every group once it becomes conscious of itself instinctively seeks other groups with which to unite to form a larger whole. Alone it cannot be effective."[32] Thus neighborhood councils are important not just for what they do in their own neighborhoods, but for evolving a larger consciousness that eventually connects it with the nation (and nations with other nations).

Arendt and Follett both accepted the practical need for representation in the sense that the meeting room cannot hold everybody once you get beyond the neighborhood level. But imagine the difference between a representative system grounded in discussions and public-spirited work among neighbors, and the one we know so well, where each isolated individual goes into a voting booth, closes the curtain, and in privacy exercises the only public responsibility and duty open to him or her.

Follett insists that she is advocating not group government but a system in which the individual can reach his or her fullest expression. Individuals are not a product of separateness but of relating.[33] The neighborhood group makes that possible. If government needs to connect to the people, as democracy does, we have to make the connection real. Individuals express only a small part of themselves in the voting booth. Genuine discussion and argument around common issues call on a part of the human being that otherwise atrophies.

It is worth noting the difference between this vision of governance and what is known as *communitarianism*. This term is used to connote bonds among members of a society that have deep historical and cultural roots, but the bonds are largely tacit and not maintained on the basis of interactions. Also, in contrast to communitarianism, the political community at the core of the Arendt–Follett model of governance is made up of people who see things differently from one another. What they have in common is a commitment to dialogue and not a set of shared values they wish to enshrine in public space. Politics is talking and arguing about common concerns, exchanging the considered opinions formed in thinking and judging issues and in listening to one another.

The vision of politics and governance is only plausible if one is willing at least to call into question the notions that human beings are primordially separate from one another and that the state of nature is a war of all against all. From these assumptions, the only stable state is one where order is imposed from above, and freedom consists of private unconstrained striving for preferred goodies. But the stable state looks different when the stability is woven from the ground up; it is plausible if you envision humans as always already connected to the world and each other.

We can come away, if we choose, from considering their ideas with at least a sense that the taken-for-granted realistic understanding of politics is not a foregone conclusion, the only possible way of imagining our common life. And if we can see this vision as chosen rather than a necessity, the door is open to what we might call governance of the common ground.[34]

GOVERNANCE OF THE COMMON GROUND

Moving forward with governance of the common ground implies giving some thought to how to do it. This form of governance may attract us for its democratic features, but how can it work? Democracy is not just a set of ideals but requires practices to support it. Making it happen requires shifting from what March and Olsen call a "logic of exchange" to a "logic of appropriateness," and then taking up the question of basic structures that reflect and nurture that logic.[35] The logic of exchange should be familiar by now. It works by means of bargaining, negotiation, and deal making. It is primarily an economic logic premised on self-interested individuals and a government that is neutral about their preferences—government as referee. There is no common will possible, only conflicts of interest that are dealt with by crafting coalitions that reach an agreement that gets the best possible results for each member. The new governance follows this logic to a great extent, fostering networks of self-interested organizational actors who come together to maximize their individual utility functions.

In contrast, the logic of appropriateness takes the idea of democratic institutions seriously. It concerns itself with governmental and other public-spirited entities in which members share democratic ideals and understand the importance of rules and practices in promoting democracy. In this institutional perspective, the relationships among actors are not just deals and coalitions that resolve conflicts among individual preferences; nor are institutions objectified, frozen entities. Rather they are patterns of practices over time, in which shared understandings develop among members about their collaborative activities. They are a form of constructed social reality, a reality constructed in interchanges among people. Institutional reality lies in the in-betweens among members.

In the institution, action is shaped, though not coerced or determined, by shared rules and understandings and by a common sense of what the situation requires. Institutional action follows norms of appropriateness constructed among members, using experience, intuition, and expertise.

The importance of thinking institutionally about active citizenship is that democratic practices need to take enabling and supportive patterns in order to perpetuate themselves. Collaboration is not just solving (or at least dealing with) one problem or issue after another. Part of the work is thinking about how to perpetuate democratic group processes and the learning that takes place. As Morse reminds us, Follett argued that "the activity must precede the form." In other words, participating ("public building") has to come first to make it possible for genuine participation to occur and then to create, participatively, institutional support that will make it lasting.[36]

The federal community health center program discussed above contains several lessons about successful governance of the common ground. First, the grant-in-aid framework institutionalized the relationship between community-based organizations and the government from the top down, so to speak, in a way that not only left room for active citizenship but mandated it. The law requires center boards of directors to consist of a majority of users of the services and empowered them with real discretionary authority. This was quite a different structure from the contract with its list of deliverables, which cares nothing for how they are produced, only for results by a date certain.

Second, once community-based organizations receive the grant funds and activities commence, people from the centers and people from the federal government have to interact with one another in order to do the required work in a mutually accountable way. These interactions construct mutual understandings about the meaning of key terms, while shared experiences build trust even though feds and citizens have differing institutional needs. This dynamic is, in effect, institutionalization from the ground up. The combination of top-down structure furnished by the enabling legislation, the grant mechanism, and a plethora of rules and protocols, with the bottom-up network of socially constructed understandings shared across organizations, has proven to be a powerful one, if the longevity of the program is any indication. A third factor is the National Association of Community Health Centers that has acted to nourish collaboration and solidarity among centers and advocated on their behalf at the national political level, which is an example of Follett's idea that representation is authentic if built from the ground up.

According to March and Olsen, democratic governance has four tasks:

- develop democratic identities of citizens and groups in the political environment;
- develop citizen, group, and institutional capacity to take action;
- develop accounts (stories) of events and actions, whose interpretations crystallize and transmit the lessons of experience in ways that promote democracy; and
- develop an adaptive political system.[37]

Based on the real-life example of the community health center program, it seems to me that there are four kinds of actions people in public service can pursue in order to promote and practice democratic governance:

- create opportunities for citizens and groups to get involved in discussing public problems, judging alternative ways of dealing with them, and working on them collaboratively;
- think seriously about structures and processes that will institutionalize citizens' civic capacity, for example, how to organize and conduct meetings that promote productive discussion, how to organize people's attention in order to alert them to neglected aspects of situations,[38] and how to perpetuate collaborative processes;
- reflect regularly and collaboratively with citizens on experiences, patterns, and trends, and mine them for lessons; and
- promote institutional learning—less rote repetition, more reflection in action.

As March and Olsen conclude, "to be a democratic citizen is to accept responsibility for crafting the practices, rules, forms, capabilities, structures, procedures, accounts, and identities that construct democratic political life."[39] Public servants, like other citizens, have a choice. The new governance is not a foregone conclusion. It is a web of understandings that actual people perpetuate in their daily lives. By the same token, governance of the common ground is not unrealistic. It is the result of many small steps—discussions, actions, stories, practices, shared understandings—in the direction of democracy.

NOTES

1. See the federal government's A-76 circular on the definition of "inherently governmental." www.whitehouse.gov/omb/circulars/a6/a76_11402.pdf. See also Larkin Dudley, "Fencing in the Inherently Governmental Debate," in *Refounding Democratic Public Administration*, ed. Gary L. Wamsley and James F. Wolf (Thousand Oaks, CA: Sage Publications, 1993), 68–91.

2. Jennifer Alexander, Renee Nank, and Camilla Stivers, "Implications of Welfare Reform: Do Survival Strategies for Nonprofits Threaten Civil Society?" *Nonprofit and Voluntary Sector Quarterly* 30 (2002).

3. For example, see Hindy Lauer Schachter, *Reinventing Government or Reinventing Ourselves: The Role of Citizen Owners in Making a Better Government* (Albany, NY: State University of New York Press, 1997).

4. See World Bank, *Sub-Saharan Africa: From Crisis to Sustainable Growth* (Washington, DC: World Bank, 1989); World Bank, *Governance and Development* (Washington, DC: World Bank, 1992).

5. Thomas Hobbes, *Leviathan*, ed. C. B. MacPherson (Harmondsworth, UK: Penguin, 1968), sec. XXI, 261.

6. Hobbes, *Leviathan*, XXI, 263.

7. Ibid., 264.

8. Ibid., 268–69.

9. Ibid., 271.

10. Hannah Arendt, *On Revolution* (Harmondsworth, UK: Penguin, 1977), 218.

11. Hannah Arendt, *Between Past and Future* (Harmondsworth, UK: Penguin, 1977), 149.

12. Arendt, *On Revolution*, 119.

13. *On Revolution*, 127.

14. *On Revolution*, 235. For an application of this idea to citizen involvement in public administration, see Ralph P. Hummel and Camilla Stivers, "Government Isn't Us," in *Government Is Us: Public Administration in an Anti-government Era*, ed. Cheryl Simrell King and Camilla Stivers (Thousand Oaks, CA: Sage Publications, 1998).

15. Hannah Arendt, *The Human Condition* (Chicago and London: University Press, 1958), 52.

16. Hannah Arendt, "Introduction into Politics," in *The Promise of Politics*, ed. Jerome Kohn (New York: Schocken Books, 2005), 95.

17. Yehezkial Dror, *The Capacity to Govern: A Report to the Club of Rome* (London and Portland, OR: Frank Cass, 2002), 3.

18. Scott Shane and Ron Nixon, "In Washington Contractors Take On Biggest Role Ever," *New York Times*, February 4, 2007, 1.

19. Robert S. Gilmour and Laura S. Jensen, "Reinventing Government Accountability: Public Functions, Privatization and the Meaning of 'State Action,'" *Public Administration Review* 58 (1998), 249, 253–54.

20. Ali Kazancigil, "Governance and Science: Market-like Modes of Managing Society and Producing Knowledge," *International Social Science Journal* 15 (1998), 72.

21. So-called realists would say that this alternative is impossible because human nature is too violent, and the modern state is too complex for face-to-face interaction. Besides, too much citizen activity would heighten political conflict and destroy the social stability on which liberty depends. Shades of Hobbes! See J. Roland Pennock, *Democratic Political Theory* (Princeton, NJ: Princeton University Press, 1979).

22. Arendt, *On Revolution*, 263.

23. Ibid., 267.

24. There are many stories of spontaneous organizing by ordinary people in the wake of Hurricane Katrina. See chapter 4.

25. For current information on community health centers, see Sara Rosenbaum and Peter Shin, "Medicaid and the Uninsured: Health Centers as Safety Net Providers," May 2003. www.kff.medicaid/loader.cfm?url=/commonsport/security/getfile/cfm&PageID=14342. See also the website for the National Association of Community Health Centers: http://nachc.org. For a summary of my research in the mid-1980s, see Camilla Stivers, "The Public Agency as Polis: Active Citizenship in the Administrative State," *Administration & Society* 22 (1990).

26. See Pradeep Chandra Kathi and Terry L. Cooper, "Democratizing the Administrative State: Connecting Neighborhood Councils and City Agencies," *Public Administration Review* 65 (2005).

27. See Keith Provan and H. Brinton Milward, "Do Networks Really Work?" *Public Administration Review* 61 (2001); and Laurence O'Toole and Kenneth J. Meier, "Desperately Seeking Selznick: Cooptation and the Dark Side of Public Management in Networks," *Public Administration Review* 63 (2003).

28. One can imagine that the city's primary initial interest was in restoring stability, but genuine democracy has a way of demonstrating its inherent value to those involved in it, regardless of what other needs it serves.

29. Mary Parker Follett, *The New State: Group Organization as the Solution of Popular Government* (University Park, PA: Pennsylvania State University Press, 1998), 204–7. Originally published 1918.

30. Follett, *The New State*, 225.

31. Ibid., 249.

32. The National Association of Community Health Centers embodies many of the features Follett envisioned in the neighborhood council system, including collaboration among community-based groups and the transmission of perspectives to broader levels of the public sphere. See note 25.

33. Ricardo S. Morse, "Prophet of Participation: Mary Parker Follett and Public Participation in Public Administration," *Administrative Theory & Praxis* 28 (2006).

34. Morse's remarkable article (note above) says that Follett's perspective on participation entails finding common ground by working together. He and I arrived independently from one another at the idea of common ground. I have learned greatly from his insightful emphasis on *work* as the crucial aspect of community building.

35. James G. March and Johan P. Olsen, *Democratic Governance* (New York: Free Press, 1995).

36. Morse, "Prophet of Participation," 11.

37. March and Olsen, *Democratic Governance*, 45–46.

38. See John Forester, "Questioning and Organizing Attention," *Administration & Society* 13 (1981).

39. March and Olsen, *Democratic Governance*, 252.

PART III

Philosophy for Practice

CHAPTER 7

Pragmatism in
Public Service

P EOPLE IN PUBLIC SERVICE TEND TO REJECT PHILOSOPHY BECAUSE
it doesn't seem to match their experience. Philosophy usually
presents truth as static—a timeless link between concept and
reality: "When you've got your true idea of anything, there's an end
of the matter. You're in possession; you know; you have fulfilled your
thinking destiny."[1] This is a point of view public servants find annoying because their lives tell them there is almost never "an end to it." The
situations they find themselves in are seldom resolved, only dealt with
in some way that enables them to move on. Pressed to measure performance, for example, they will find a measurement and a method they
can live with for the time being, one that at least holds out hope for
learning something useful about the program in question, one that will
satisfy those to whom they are accountable. But they rarely conclude
that performance measurement—or any other form of systematic investigation—gives an end to the matter.

In contrast to the search for unchanging truth, pragmatism asks,
"Grant an idea or belief to be true . . . what concrete difference will
its being true make in anyone's actual life? . . . What experiences will be
different from those which would obtain if the belief were false?"[2] In
the measurement of administrative performance, the real test comes not
when the measurement quantifies program results but afterward, when
administrators experience what might be called "the results of the results." What difference does it make in practice when we know that only

50 percent of the children in a certain school measured up to the norm on a standardized test? What impact does that knowledge have on our understanding of the situation in that school? What changes in teaching strategies does it trigger? How does it affect the self-images of the children and therefore their willingness and ability to learn? What steps do top administrators take to improve the chances for better results next time? Are the results of the results, the impact of the measurements on future actions, *the ones we want?* That is, does measuring performance in a certain way actually improve education?

The point—or at least one important point—of performance measurement is to improve performance. Thus, the pragmatists would say, there is a real sense in which knowledge such as the kind produced by a standardized test only becomes "true" when we experience what happens after we get the test results. Do they actually help us improve how children learn? As William James said, "The truth of an idea [like performance measurement] is not a stagnant property. . . . Truth *happens* to an idea. It becomes true, is made true by events."[3] For pragmatism, there is no such thing as an idea that is good in theory but doesn't work in practice. Performance measurement may be a good theory, but its goodness can only be validated in practice—not in terms of whether the tests themselves produce valid data, though that's a start, but in terms of whether the activities of testing and the activities the data lead to are judged to be useful in doing the work out of which performance comes. We need the life results to talk back to the test results.

Pragmatism as described by early twentieth-century American writers starts from the premise that the truth of a thought is tested in action, which should be an appealing idea for practicing administrators. William James once said that ideas *become* true "just in so far as they help us to get into satisfactory relation with other parts of our experience."[4] This turns out to be as rich a notion as any philosophy has produced.

In contrast, the kind of pragmatism that permeates today's public sector thinking is a form of the hard-nosed realism we have already discussed, which sets aside principles for the sake of getting things done, "Well, it would be nice to consider right and wrong, or the letter of the law, but we can't afford such niceties, we have to be pragmatic." The underlying message of this tough-minded approach is that searching for the good or the true doesn't get you where you have to go. But there is another sort of pragmatism, one that combines a respect for hands-on experience with a commitment to emergent truth and goodness. On this basis, it qualifies as philosophy for practice.

When practitioners are urged to consult philosophy, as sometimes happens in public administration classes, the common (though usually tacit) reaction is, "We don't have time for this, let's get on with putting out the next fire." Philosopher John Dewey was completely familiar with this attitude, noting "Philosophy, [the critics] say, is circular and disputatious; it settles nothing." Philosophers debate the same questions endlessly, but science "settles some things and moves on to others." So the critics "conclude that while philosophy is a form of knowledge or science, it is a pretentious and pseudo-form, an effort at a kind of knowledge which is impossible."[5]

Dewey refused to give in to the notion that philosophy is at best an impractical indulgence. He encourages us to think about philosophy not as a form of knowledge but "a love . . . of wisdom . . . a social hope reduced to a working program of action . . . disciplined by serious thought and knowledge."[6] In other words, doing philosophy is not about coming up with final answers. It is an unending, caring quest, a commitment to the practice of thinking in a systematic way about important questions without the promise of settling them once and for all, a testing of ideas in practice, a search for the results of the results.

Public administrators, as people who are charged with such care and seldom if ever reach the point where an issue or task is completely settled, should find such a quest familiar. Much of public administration, indeed all public sector work, may aim for final answers to complex questions, but few people in public life are ever sure they have reached even one of them. As such a commitment to a life in public administration is much like a commitment to studying philosophy, at least to the extent that such a life is pursued with as much systematic reflection as possible. Both are grounded in ambiguity tolerated for the sake of something deeper. In this case, philosophy in public service fits the nature of administrative practice better than the push to find the technical tool or strategy that produces the biggest bang for the buck.

According to Dewey philosophy uses knowledge to think deeply, but it is not itself a type of knowledge. A public administrator might draw on knowledge such as socioeconomic data or public opinion polls. He or she may think through what course of action to take or to recommend to a policymaker, but the result of that reflection is not more knowledge but judgment—debatable, marked more by its aspiration to wisdom than by proof that it counts as wisdom. "All deliberate action of mind is in a way an experiment with the world to see what it will stand for, what it will promote and what frustrate."[7] For Dewey, as for pragmatism generally, philosophy is not something done away from life in ivory towers but in the thick of things. Far from being impractical or out of touch with real life, it is pursued in the midst of the most down-to-earth situations. It fits, in other words, the practice of public administration.

Experience

Jane Addams, founder of Chicago's Hull House, once wrote that the settlement house was "an attempt to express the meaning of life in terms of life itself, in forms of activity."[8] The same might be said of the public or nonprofit agency today, despite the push to demonstrate results. The meaning of the work is produced in the work itself by the people in the situation, as they experience it. In this sense, defining and measuring results will help improve performance only if the defining and the measuring emerge from the work itself—from the know-how of the people involved in it, both service providers and citizens. As Mary Parker Follett said, "No more fatally disastrous conception has ever dominated us than the concept of static ends."[9] Ends emerge and develop through experience.

Imposing performance measurement from outside the situation requires everyone to live up to an abstraction rather than creating meaning in experience. Does matching up to an abstraction really achieve political accountability? The market model of public service, from which the emphasis on performance measurement comes, assumes that accountability consists in measuring what we can measure or what we choose to measure, rather than in addressing what citizens themselves have learned from experience is important about the particular service in question. Agency managers need to step "out of the managerial zone of control into territory where the relationship between what providers do and what citizens want is unknown, and [try] to create value there."[10]

The idea that agencies should create value for all their stakeholders is a popular one in recent days. It's a useful notion because it encourages us to think of values not as pre-existing substances leaders can use as sources of energy for agency work (as in the notion of "mission-driven," which gives a mental picture of the mission as a kind of gasoline to make the organizational engine run). Rather, values are created experientially in the process of the work. Dewey advised much the same viewpoint when he wrote: "The conclusion is not that value is subjective, but that it is practical. . . . There is no value save in situations where desires and the need of deliberation in order to choose are found. . . . Reflection is a process of finding out what we want. . . . In this process, things *get* values."[11] It is in the experience of the work itself that we are able to create its meaning. The only pragmatic recommendation to make in the idea of creating value *for* stakeholders is that we create value *with* them. Values are not injected like a vitamin shot into shared experience, rather they grow out of it.

THE TASK OF ONWARDNESS

The pragmatic view of truth as emerging from experience contrasts sharply with the view I criticized earlier, in which fully formed truth lies hidden underneath appearances waiting to be discovered (chapter 2). Pragmatism's emphasis on experience implies a universe whose operations are contingent. Just as in pragmatism there are no fixed, final truths, so there is also no static reality out there waiting for us to find it. Pragmatists are suspicious of absolutes, iron laws, immovable boundaries. The concepts people employ to fix reality, to make it stand still, have come out of experience—indeed, where else could they come from? Experience is always on the move; therefore the fix is always temporary. Ralph Waldo Emerson once observed that his objection to empiricism was not its experience base but its limited understanding of experience as fixed and predictable. He was impatient with philosophy's obsession with the conflict between reality-as-out-there versus reality-as-constructed; subjectivity versus objectivity; inner versus outer. In his view, these pointless conflicts ought to give way to "the task of onward-ness"—that is, acknowledging that most of life consists in moving on rather than settling down, and acting on that recognition.[12] This emphasis on human life as movement rather than something static is another aspect of pragmatism that seems to fit the practice of public administration.

The task of onwardness entails the willingness to live with ambigu-ity—something people in public life learn as raw recruits. Most come to public service out of a desire to make things better, but experience teaches them that small victories are to be savored because big ones are extremely rare. The challenge, they find, is to avoid either pretending the ambiguity doesn't exist or succumbing to pessimism or apathy. This is a different sort of realism, by the way, from the familiar one. Accept-ing ambiguity and celebrating small wins are not the same thing at all as spending your life cynically expecting the worst of everybody and building a defensive wall around the few hopes you haven't abandoned entirely.

Take the case of Beverlee Myers, whose life in public service culmi-nated in serving as director of California's Department of Public Health during the Jerry Brown administration. Throughout her career, Myers grounded her work in a vision of the immense potential power of fed-eral funding to improve health care delivery rather than simply support it in its current form. Instead of paying doctors and hospitals to go on supplying patients with whatever care the professionals thought best, Myers believed health policy could use the power of public dollars to encourage (or require) practices that would bring better health care to people who couldn't afford it. Yet time and again she ran into political walls that kept this dream of transformation from being achieved. When she headed the California Health Department, she became embroiled in a heated dispute with the State Medical Society over delays in Medi-Cal reimbursements. The controversy shoved aside all other issues and left Myers bruised by the criticisms of legislators responding to the powerful medical lobby. Yet she still had the energy to refuse Governor Jerry Brown's order to develop a nuclear disaster plan, on the grounds that a plan would give citizens the false impression that a nuclear attack could be coped with. And she overcame decades of ill feeling between her department and a network of county health departments so that real intergovernmental collaboration could begin.[13]

Myers's life reflects what a poet once called "wild patience." The wildness showed itself in her energetic refusal to accept the notion that the nation's health system could not be improved, particularly for poor people; her willingness to speak out; and her ability to pick herself up after a bruising battle and keep going. The patience is reflected in her recognition of the nature and extent of the opposition she faced, her keen sense of strategy, and her careful attention to administrative responsibilities. Beverlee Myers understood the task of onwardness.

In a life like Myers's can be seen John Dewey's open-ended understanding of growth and development. He rejected the idea of growth as steady movement toward a culmination of tendencies that were there from the beginning. Developing human potential is not a matter of cultivating or bringing out qualities that a person was born with. We cannot know what those potentialities are until they are brought out in interactions with the world—in experience. Thus human nature is simply an open question. The individuality of each person is not lying there like a seed waiting to sprout. The form it takes depends on the circumstances encountered in experience—in the process of onwardness. There is no way of knowing what Beverlee Myers's individuality would have been without specific events, past history, and personalities that shaped her life. It shines forth in her actions.

Individuality, in fact, is contingent. As such it is "the source of whatever is unpredictable in the world."[14] Myers's response to a particular situation could not have been predicted with certainty even with complete knowledge of her genetic make-up, upbringing, education, and experience to date. People who knew her well no doubt did predict from time to time how she would handle a problem—but sometimes they were wrong. Dewey held that "it is a mystery that anything which exists is just what it is."[15] And at the heart of the mystery is the uniqueness of each individual, for which no science can account. Ernest Becker said it this way: "We don't know where babies come from. You get married, you're sitting at a table having breakfast—there are two of you—and a year later there's somebody else, sitting there. And if you're honest with yourself, you don't know where [that somebody] came from."[16]

Hannah Arendt built a political philosophy around this idea of the mystery of individuality. She called it "natality" out of a sense that with the birth of each human being something completely new comes into the world: "Nobody is ever the same as anyone else who ever lived, lives, or will live."[17] Although she was not a declared pragmatist, Arendt's emphasis on individual uniqueness matches the pragmatic emphasis on development quite well: The life process is emergent rather than pre-defined. Arendt regarded the very notion of human nature as misguided because it wipes out individual uniqueness in its concentration on the ways in which we are all alike. Human beings are fundamentally *plural*, and political freedom consists in public action and speech in which each of us (often without fully meaning to) shows others who (not what) he or she is.

Efforts to generalize about human nature or to control the dynamics of public life are antipolitical because they blot out the newness that each of us brings into the world. This newness—the uniqueness of each individual—is what makes human interaction ultimately unpredictable. Patterns are visible at the macro level but they have blurred boundaries. At the micro level, the level of the individual or the small group, creativity—the task of onwardness from which contingent and temporary truths emerge—overwhelms the effort to predict and control. This view of human action matches the view of public service as an ongoing practice, a process rather than a set of static techniques.

Considered from the pragmatic view of reality as emergent, public administration looks less solid than the image it presents to the world. The fabric of interactions among agency members escapes the most energetic efforts to assert full control, and programmatic results seldom match predicted values. Researchers inside and outside agencies measure what is measurable; meanwhile, most of the dynamics of administrative life are never captured—not only because many researchers are relatively uninterested in what they can't pin down numerically, but also because interpersonal relations can only be imperfectly observed. The shared assumptions, the tacit rules, go largely unnoticed—at least until they are breached.

People who work in agencies tend to be all too aware of the written rules that impinge on their every move, yet the gap between each rule and how an administrator applies it guarantees newness in the most outwardly rigid setting. There is no rule for applying a rule. The application has to be worked out in practice, using the judgment agency members have acquired in experience. And because each member is a unique individual, and each situation different from all the others, the way things work out in practice can't be predicted. Then, too, the working out is not so much a closure as it is another beginning, an opening into the future. No wonder Dewey called pragmatism a philosophy of courage, "the courage to venture into the unknown."[18]

THE COMMUNITY OF INQUIRY

So far pragmatism seems to be a rather slippery, shifting basis for public sector practice. Despite the central place of life experience, there is something frustrating about a guide to public life that so roundly resists being solidified. Downplaying abstractions and theories has undeniable appeal to people struggling to cope with conflicting demands and multiple accountabilities. Still, those same demands and accountabilities give rise to a certain longing to know that there is something underneath it all that can serve as a reference point, a ground—if not to stand firmly on, at least to move forward from.

Pragmatism does offer a ground of sorts, though it is more of a process than a structure. As we have seen knowledge is fallible, subject to modification as it is applied. Every knowledge claim is open to being tested and criticized. As pragmatist Charles Sanders Peirce said, science requires "a community of inquirers, whose discovery of reality in the long run requires that its current practice be governed by consensus."[19] In other words, any process of inquiry requires a set of ground rules for conducting the inquiry and evaluating the results. It is not that there are no standards for judging factual or moral assertions. There are, but they are not sitting outside somewhere on a cloud. Rather they are debated in communities that form out of interest in and/or commitment to a particular project or focus. "The pragmatists highlighted the priority of the intersubjective social and communal dimensions of experience, language and inquiry."[20] They saw knowledge of reality as constructed in a social process of deliberation in which the standards, norms, and rules of thumb applied to a problem or question were themselves the products of previous communities of inquiry, selected, tested, and modified in the process at hand.

This view of knowledge as based on interaction led John Dewey to the idea that democracy was the only mode of public life that matched the knowledge process. The requirement that our knowledge and value claims do not have transcendental grounds but have to be argued about and discussed is a view of the knowledge process as a kind of democracy. "No government by experts in which the masses do not have the chance to inform the experts as to their needs can be anything but an oligarchy managed in the interests of the few."[21]

The suggestion that knowledge is democratic sounds outlandish at first. After all, do we decide what is true by majority vote? According to Dewey, "Many persons seem to suppose that facts carry their meaning along with themselves on their face. Accumulate enough of them and their interpretation stares out at you."[22] I ran into this belief years ago interviewing dozens of public health practitioners in the course of a national study. Many people the study team talked to said something like, "Public health is a science, science gives us the facts, and the facts tell us what to do." Obviously, these professionals didn't believe that knowledge was democratic, or maybe it would be more accurate to say that they saw no difference between knowledge and possession of facts.[23] But there is a gap between facts and knowledge, one that has to be bridged by means of deliberation.

The meaning of facts, what they imply for understanding public problems and deciding what to do about them, is never obvious on its face. The conversion of facts into knowledge can only be done through interpretation, debate, discussion, and persuasion. This process of coming to understand situations and issues should be as open and inclusive as possible. Dewey's criticism of traditional philosophy applies equally to the knowledge systems that currently shape public life, which are wedded to the view that some forms of knowledge are inherently superior to others. That commitment makes them claim the authority to make their knowledge definitive. As Dewey pointed out, this is a deeply undemocratic idea. Making definite knowledge claims has the effect of shutting off debate, whereas politics *is* debate; therefore knowledge claims such as those made by science are antipolitical.

Dewey thought that scientists and other "highbrows" needed to keep in mind that all human beings are experts on the conditions of their own lives. This doesn't mean that all of us know all we need to about our problems and the problems of our communities. What we do know, however, has the kind of validity that comes only out of direct experience—out of living. We can add to that knowledge or we can reinterpret it; that is, we can learn. But wrestling with public problems and deciding on courses of action to deal with them has to start from what people know from daily life.

It is amazing how frequently experts underrate or even ignore what people know about a situation just from living in it. A few days after September 11, 2001, a *New York Times* story carried this headline, "Even workers can see flaws in airlines' screening system."[24] *Even* workers! Why is this such a surprise? Who would know the flaws in the system better than the screeners themselves? Yet until disaster struck no one asked them how things were going, and of course overworked and poorly paid people were hardly going to volunteer information, especially when they were likely to get blamed for whatever was wrong.

What if, instead of investigating the screeners, someone had asked them to help figure out ways to improve the system? Out of direct experience and facts amassed through scientific study, people build democratic knowledge by means of discussion and argument. Yet this is rarely done. Somebody has to take the fall, after all. One difficulty with the American representative system of government is that it provides few pipelines for conveying people's lived experiences into the policy process, whether they are firing line workers, like the airport screeners, clients of the service delivery system, or citizens in general.

Dewey's view of knowledge acquisition as a community process made him see democracy as "the faith that the process of experience is more important than any special result attained. . . . Democracy as compared with other ways of life is the sole way of living which believes wholeheartedly in the process of experience as ends and means."[25] Democracy is a way of life, not just a political or governmental system;

politics can't be separated from the rest of life. Forms of life are implicated in forms of government and vice versa.

When it comes down to it, no matter how much supporting data, what firm rules of evidence, or how rigorous our methodologies, in a democracy there is "nothing to which we can ultimately appeal" in making the case for a policy or an administrative move except "the experiences and understandings of our fellow citizens."[26] The recognition that the tests of our proposals are conducted not in theory but in life makes principled advocacy a core responsibility of public service. We have to turn to others in a wider community of inquiry than the one in which a particular proposal was crafted and try to get them to buy into our idea.

Dewey believed that inquiry starts when people run up against a problem. Because public service is "just one thing after another," we don't have to look far to run up against problems. But the implication is that each problematic situation is unique. The situation wouldn't be a problem if it weren't. If we had encountered the same thing before, we would smoothly move through the necessary steps without much if any reflection on what to do. So, a problem is *new*. If this is the case, then the community of inquiry that forms, or can form, around each problem is also unique. This means that one way to start (consciously) being pragmatic in public life is at the level of the problem. We don't need systemwide implementation in order to become pragmatic. As Fred Thayer, a former U.S. Army official-turned-philosopher once advised me, "Never try to solve a problem sitting alone in your cubicle. Go out and talk to other people." In other words, initiate a process of inquiry.

Second, the question of who's in the community of inquiry has to be addressed. Most such communities in public life today are made up of experts—scientists, managers, analysts, and so on—whether in administrative agencies or on legislative staffs. The pragmatic attitude about inquiry is that it needs experts, but it also needs the involvement of as many constituencies as possible—whoever will be affected by the decision. This includes members of the general public. The question, then, is, Who should be included and how do we get them involved? In particular, how do we make it possible for people to join in on an equal footing?

A third question is, How wide should the community's range of considerations be? Is the problem one that requires us only to consider short-range consequences and/or a narrow range of interests, or does the discussion need to be more far-reaching? This question has implications not only for who should be included but at what point. The issue of what the inquiry is going to cover is not one without democratic implications, for the decision about the expansiveness of the discussion may mean the inclusion or exclusion of certain constituencies.

Yet another important question has to do with the deliberative process itself. Most people who have not been trained in conflict resolution or organizational development have little if any idea that there are methods to improve the chances of having a productive discussion. Many have been trained in professional disciplines that socialized them into viewing conversations as contests, so they go into a discussion aiming to shut it down rather than encourage it (for example, by scoring points and winning). Then, too, most of us work in some sort of hierarchical structure where there are rules about who can say what to whom, especially without penalty. Such circumstances shape what people are able and willing to say in a supposedly free discussion, so conscious steps have to be taken to make the process as open as possible.

Despite these real barriers there are more opportunities for experimenting with communities of inquiry than are being tapped right now. The idea of inquiry as a democratic process is not one that requires perfect preexisting conditions, whatever one might imagine those to be. Pragmatism would advise public servants to start where they are and see what is possible.

PHILOSOPHY FOR PRACTICE

What kind of ground for practice, then, does pragmatism offer? Or better, how could we turn it into a way of doing work in the public sector? How do experience, onwardness, and community come together to provide a grounding for administrative practice? A summary of the argument follows.

In pragmatism, experience is the test of a truth. The pragmatic administrator asks what difference a belief, fact, or analysis makes to the situation at hand. Does it move the situation in a positive direction? This question, by the way, is not the same thing as demanding that the truths that come out of experience be the ones we want. Sometimes situations talk back, they tell us things we don't like hearing but must hear if our purposes are to be moved forward. The pragmatic administrator tests knowledge in new experience, experimenting with possibilities and learning from what happens. This process is useful even when the answer experience gives back is one we would rather not get.

Testing truth requires that we acknowledge that reality is not static—it moves. Our purposes enable us to define situations creatively, not dissolve all ambiguity. The pragmatic administrator accepts the inevitability of ambiguity and celebrates small wins. Administrative action is creative, not predictive. By and large, control (such as that required to guarantee results) is an illusion. Dark times teach us this. Pragmatism is a form of courage, of resoluteness and hope in the face of the unknown. At the same time it is a developmental practice through which individual uniqueness emerges.

Finally, in a fluid and unpredictable universe, the one really practical foundation is the one offered in communities of inquiry. This sort of inquiry lies at the core of governance of the common ground. The pragmatic administrator looks for opportunities to generate democratic processes of inquiry in which guidance for inquiry—and simultaneously guidance for practice—is created in the process itself. As Mary Parker Follett said, individual creativity is most fully expressed "when all 'wishes' unite in a working whole."[27] Even within the overtly static hierarchies of the public bureaucracy, community processes of inquiry are flowing. Pragmatism requires not a transformation of reality but a change in awareness so that action can be consciously creative, and a change in approach, so that inquiry can be democratic.

All of the above is hardly new. It is only meant to suggest that pragmatism in public service does not require a sea change before it can be practiced, though the more we experiment with reflection in action along pragmatic lines, the more likely positive creativity is to occur. Democratizing the dynamics of public life is an incremental process that does not require donning rose-colored spectacles. There is a difference between cockeyed optimism and what Dewey called "social hope."

Public service will go on being a demanding way to spend your life, one that requires courage in the face of the unknown, but one with newly vital meaning.

NOTES

1. William James, "Pragmatism's Conception of the Truth," in *Pragmatism: A Reader*, ed. Louis Menand (New York: Vintage Books, 1997), 113. Originally published in 1907.

2. James, "Pragmatism's Conception of the Truth," 113–14.

3. Ibid., 114.

4. William James, "What Pragmatism Means," in Menand, 100. Originally published in 1907.

5. John Dewey, "Philosophy and Democracy," in *The Essential Dewey, Volume I: Pragmatism, Education, Democracy*, ed. Larry A. Hickman and Thomas M. Alexander (Bloomington and Indianapolis, IN: Indiana University Press, 1998), 72. Originally published in 1919.

6. Dewey, "Philosophy and Democracy," 72–73.

7. Ibid., 75.

8. Jane Addams, "A Function of the Social Settlement," in Menand, 276. Originally published in 1899.

9. Mary Parker Follett, "Community Is a Process," *Philosophical Review* 28 (1919), 579.

10. Janet Kelly, "The Dilemma of the Unsatisfied Customer," *Public Administration Review* 55 (2005), 82.

11. John Dewey, "The Logic of Judgments of Practice," in *The Essential Dewey, Volume II: Ethics, Logic, Psychology*," ed. Larry A. Hickman and Thomas Alexander (Bloomington and Indianapolis, IN: Indiana University Press, 1998), 246.

12. Stanley Cavell, "Thinking of Emerson," in Cavell, *Emerson's Transcendental Etudes*, ed. David Justin Hodge (Palo Alto, CA: Stanford University Press, 2003), 19.

13. Camilla Stivers, "Beverlee A. Myers: Power, Virtue, and Womanhood in Public Administration," in *Exemplary Public Administrators: Character and Leadership in Government*, ed. Terry L. Cooper and N. Dale Wright (San Francisco, CA: Jossey-Bass, 1992).

14. John Dewey, "Time and Individuality," in On Experience, Nature and Freedom, ed. Richard J. Bernstein (Indianapolis, IN: Bobbs-Merrill, 1960), 240.

15. Ibid.

16. Quoted in Robert Kramer, "Otto Rank and 'The Cause'," typescript from the author, 1997, 23.

17. Hannah Arendt, *The Human Condition* (Chicago: University of Chicago Press, 1958), 8.

18. Naoko Saito, "Pragmatism and the Tragic Sense," *Journal of Philosophy of Education* 36 (2002), 254.

19. Charles Sanders Peirce, "Some Consequences of Four Incapacities," quoted in James Bohman, "Democracy as Inquiry, Inquiry as Democracy: Pragmatism, Social Science, and the Cognitive Division of Labor," *American Journal of Political Science* 43 (1999), 591.

20. Richard J. Bernstein, "The Resurgence of Pragmatism," *Social Research* 59 (1992), 814.

21. Quoted in Eric A. MacGilvray, "Experience as Experiment: Some Consequences of Pragmatism in Democratic Theory," *American Journal of Political Science* 43 (1999), 561.

22. John Dewey, "Search for the Public," in Hickman and Alexander Volume I, 281. Originally published 1927.

23. Camilla Stivers, "The Politics of Public Health: The Dilemma of a Public Profession," in *Health Politics and Policy*, 2nd ed., ed. Theodor Litman and Leonard Robins (Delmar, 1990).

24. Steven Greenhouse and Christopher Drew, "After the Attacks: Airport Security; Even Workers Can See Flaws in Airlines' Screening System," *New York Times*, September 14, 2001.

25. John Dewey, "Democracy as a Moral Ideal," quoted in *Pragmatism: The Classic Writings*, ed. H. S. Thayer (Indianapolis, IN: Hackett, 1982), 261.

26. MacGilvray, "Experience as Experiment," 563.

27. Follett, "Community Is a Process," 567.

CHAPTER 8

Public Service Ethics in Dark Times

P UBLIC SERVICE FACES DOUBLY DARK TIMES. THROUGH A philosophical lens we have shed some light on what it means, in these times, to reason, think, and judge; the nature of truth; alternative models of governance and their implications for democracy. For now the question that remains concerns the relevance of ethics for leading a meaningful life in public service.

People in public service often think of ethics as a matter of adhering to rules and codes. Members of my ethics classes say rules and codes of ethics are important because they present clear guidelines and set firm limits around acceptable behavior. In some ways this view is persuasive. If it is not written down somewhere that it's unethical to let a potential contractor take you out to lunch—let alone buy you a membership in the local country club—then some people, at least, will think that anything goes. At least that is the view expressed by many practitioners I talk to. On the other hand, news stories about ethics violations regularly show that some people will think anything goes no matter how many rules and codes there are.

Well-crafted rules and codes, and behavior that faithfully follows them, only scratch the surface of public service ethics. In a way, rules and codes are the "CYA" level of ethics (politely, "cover your anatomy"). You follow them just in case someone decides to launch an investigation. But there is so much more to public service than refusing bribes or not taking pens home from the office. Too much writing on ethics in the public sector is directed at issues like abuse of sick leave that are labor-management concerns.

Another ethical focus is the way public servants use administrative discretion. Laws and regulations, no matter how clear, still leave a lot of room for interpretation in particular situations. Does a particular client qualify for certain benefits? Does this tract of land count as a wetland? Most applicants don't fit neatly into the benefit guidelines, and no piece of land matches the textbook definition of a wetland exactly. These decisions require weighing whether or not the situation fits the rule.

How should such assessments be made? In a famous debate launched more than fifty years ago, one side argued that administrators could and should simply follow the law and legislative intent. The counterargument was they should look to professional standards and a sense of how the public would react to a particular decision. Neither side ever questioned whether administrative discretion is the central ethical issue in public service; the debate (or more accurately the ensuing decades of dialogue around it) simply took center stage in administrative ethics dialogue and has been there ever since.

Is the issue of administrative discretion important to public service ethics? Clearly it is. Administrators are constantly called upon to decide about issues great and small, which have real consequences for members of the public. This is still true despite the farming out of so much service delivery, and the transfer of discretionary power that goes with it, to the private sector. Perhaps it is even truer than it used to be. The basis now for such decision making is not the only thing in question. The public also has to wonder where the buck stops. Yet there may be even more to public service ethics than this.

There is another angle from which to look at ethics, one that at first may seem strange. It comes from the belief that practices of governing in dark times require new perspectives. My argument is that we should consider ethical practice for its effect on personal development. If this sounds selfish at first, I hope to persuade you that it isn't. To the contrary, it may be the core of public service that will carry us through dark times. The idea comes from several thinkers already discussed, especially John Dewey and Michel Foucault. Despite their considerable differences, they thought that the core of ethics, and therefore

of living, has to do with self-development. To place public service ethics in context, we need to start with a few thoughts on the nature of
government.

GOVERNING

No matter how removed any particular public servant is from contact
with particular clients or citizens, his or her work flows into the larger
enterprise of governing. Contract management is governing others, just
as much as guarding prisoners, managing a public housing complex, or
treating patients at a public health clinic. Collecting and analyzing
census data or intelligence data, deciding which neighborhoods a new
highway is going to go through, being first on the scene after a disaster,
teaching schoolchildren—all count as activities of governing.

In all the aspects of government work, two forces are entwined:
knowledge and power. The rise of specific technical knowledge can be
traced to the transformation of the state from the personal possession
of a sovereign to an institution whose purpose is to protect and care
for its citizens. Once governing started to be about something other
than the person of the sovereign ("the prince"), it required collecting
and analyzing information about the population in order for the state
to be effective in carrying out its primary duties. The word "statistics"
dates from the emergence of the state's need for accurate knowledge.[1]

Knowledge without power, however, is helpless. The state has to have
the power to shape its population and the factors impinging on it so
that society runs well. Citizens become, in a sense, natural resources for
the fashioning of an effective state. Bringing knowledge effectively to
bear requires means-ends calculations, which put statistical information
and analysis to work to achieve the goals of the state. Governing is no
longer about the prince and his personal skills and wisdom (or lack of
them); now it is about knowledge and power as they are put into practice by a governing apparatus.

Today's education for public service reflects the intertwined dynamics of knowledge and power. Policy analysis, statistics, research methods,
management, organizational behavior, public health, public works, social
work, planning—these are the skills and topics necessary for effective

governing to stabilize, regulate, and enhance social processes. Ethics is certainly a part of the curriculum more often than not, but the focus is more likely to be on aspects that make knowledge and power effective: avoiding corruption, adhering to professional standards, marshaling the knowledge necessary to make the most effective decision—the one most likely to get results consistent with established values.

Michel Foucault traces these developments. He emphasizes that the shift from sovereignty to what he called "governmentality" is a shift from a self-contained, individual practice to one that consists of a web of means-ends calculations.[2] It involves "the cross-fertilizing interplay between different agencies and expertises, private and public alike . . . the propensity of the public institutions of government to secrete within themselves their own multiple spaces of partly autonomous authority; the different forms of delegation represented by the [non-governmental organization], municipal privatization and the renewed mobilization of the voluntary sector in social services."[3] The knowledge and techniques of governing are carried on in government agencies, nonprofit and voluntary organizations and networks, and other interfaces between government agencies and the organizations to which they have "devolved" authority, to use the term popular today.

Because so much of governing entails making society run smoothly, the need for expertise is paramount. Professionals must bring their knowledge and skills to bear to develop and maintain governing capacity, to identify social problems, investigate and classify populations, control deviance, develop and implement workable social policies, and staff problem-solving organizations. The fact that many of these governing professionals work in organizations outside government does not change the importance of their work to societal stability and state capacity.

Professional expertise is in fact a crucial resource for the modern state. But it is a mixed blessing. First, professionals tend to assume that the kind of knowledge they possess is not only necessary but outweighs other knowledges in importance—for example, the knowledge ordinary people have about the conditions of their lives. Second, as Foucault showed, government professionals play a major role in shaping the self-understandings of the state's citizens. They shape us as clients of government, recipients of benefits, applicants for permits, taxpayers, students, patients, prisoners, foster children and parents, payers of child support, users of recreation facilities, residents of public housing, and so on. Residents of modern states derive a lot of their sense of self from their relationships to government; according to Foucault, the point of the activities of governing is to encourage people to understand themselves in ways that promote their obedience to the state. He insists, however, if that were all there is to governing, we could simplistically conclude that government oppresses everyone. That aspect is not all there is to it: "We need to escape from the dilemma of being either for or against. One can, after all, be face to face [with a government], and upright. Working with a government doesn't imply either a subjection or a blanket acceptance. One can work and be intransigent at the same time. I would even say that the two things go together."[4]

The implications for today's public servants are twofold. As you practice the knowledge and skills of governing, recognize how much power you wield and the impact it has on people's lives, but also recognize how much room there is to think differently. Foucault's argument is not a simplistic indictment of the administrative state, although it is clearly critical. The problem is not so much bureaucratic organizational form itself as it is bureaucrats who don't reflect, who don't maintain some distance between the jobs they have been given to do, the power that is theirs to exercise, and their own sense of themselves. Recall the question from chapter 1, "How can the growth of capabilities be disconnected from the intensification of power relations?" It asks, How can public servants improve and exercise their expertise in ways that resist taking advantage of and enhancing their own power? Let's take a look at the self and the origins of power.

Dewey and the Moral Self

How do we fulfill the obligation to resist aggrandizing the power of public professionalism? It requires an internal dialogue and maintaining distance from assigned roles and mandates. John Dewey said that the decisions we make reveal who we are and shape who we will be. When we make a choice we are not just choosing this or that course of action, we are also choosing what kind of person we are going to be in the future.[5] In that sense every action in public service is also a step in one direction or another for the shaping of the self.

Awareness of the implications of on-the-job actions not just for policy implementation but for the shape of the self is not what the economists call a utility-maximizing action. As I argued earlier, assuming that all human action is self-interested is just that: an assumption, a point of departure that forms further questions, not an empirically demonstrated proposition. Dewey argued that it was silly to think of all human action as "self-interested." Of course there is a self involved in every human action. The question is, what kind of self?[6] Many of our actions are unreflective, spontaneous. We acquire them by habit or upbringing or original temperament. In this sense they may be self-interested more often than not. (Even here, though, someone like New Yorker Wesley Autry, who had only a few seconds to make up his mind to jump in front of a subway train to rescue a fallen stranger, should give us pause.) Reflective choice, however, is generally different. The situations we encounter in which various factors clash, and we are forced to stop and consider before we make up our minds are most compelling. "We prefer spontaneously, we choose deliberately, knowingly."[7] Thus even if it is the case that all preferences are "self-ish," a notion Dewey rejects, deliberation rises above them through the use of judgment.

As previous chapters argue, self always exists in relationship to other selves. No self is ever completely isolated, which means that independent judgment, reflectivity, personal integrity, and initiative are not only individual traits but social attributes. Government of others and government of the self are intertwined. Governing will be carried forward most judiciously when public servants think for themselves and carry on an internal dialogue—even if they end up toeing the line. It is better you know what the right action is though you may not be able to carry it out. As my friend and colleague Ken Dolbeare used to tell our students at The Evergreen State College, if you don't know the difference between what you've been ordered to do and what you would do if you could, then you are just a hired gun.

Fundamentally, then, ethics in public service, in governing, comes down to a silent dialogue between me and myself, in which I figure out whether my actions are in agreement with my best sense of myself (cf., chapter 3). The point is to know what you believe to be the case and speak that truth when you can.

PERSONAL DEVELOPMENT

Public service that promotes the freedom of citizens and public servants alike entails consideration of personal development or the concern for the self's relationship to itself as well as to others. Ethics is a way of being rather than adherence to rules or precepts, or making a string of decisions. It has two aspects: first, refusal to accept whole cloth the identity handed to you by others (whether the source is schooling, therapeutic diagnosis and advice, professional standards, or job descriptions); second, willingness to discover new aspects of your identity as they arise out of your practice. Learn to think for yourself, question accepted wisdom, and reflect on events and on your own actions. The point is to be willing to escape the boundaries of inherited or externally imposed identities. How this might happen depends on circumstances. "The liberty to transgress . . . differs for the philosopher, the head of state, or the bureaucrat . . . [It involves] struggle according to one's unique rootedness in the world and history . . . a struggle for freedom within the confines of a historical situation."[8]

Clearly personal development sometimes (though not always) takes the form of action against the mandates one has been handed. Foucault called this sort of action "transgression." He believed it was important for all of us to be willing to explore the limits within which we ordinarily move and experiment with the possibility of going beyond them. Public servants sometimes do this:

- Bunnatine Greenhouse, a senior career employee of the U.S. Army Corps of Engineers, refused to approve noncompetitive contracts to a subsidiary of Halliburton far in excess of the allowable amounts. Her protest stated she believed that the integrity of the contracting process had broken down. She was reassigned to an innocuous job but not before her courageous actions brought the practice to the attention of Congress.[9]

- At the Federal Aviation Administration, Debra Srite found that among the fifty-eight contracts awarded to one company were unexplained and unallowable expenses (trips to Las Vegas, a Porsche lease). The company was submitting invoices electronically on an FAA contract management website. Even though she was the contracting officer, Srite had to ask program managers for the password. When she discovered that a top FAA official had required the company to hire his wife and ordered it to keep her on the payroll even after the contract ended, Srite reported a possible ethics violation to the FAA's legal counsel. "It's our personal obligation, especially when representing our government, to represent the public interest," she said, adding that she would not be surprised if her career suffered as a result.[10]

- Beverlee Myers, the public health official encountered in chapter 7, resigned in protest from her post as New York State's Medicaid program director because severe cuts imposed by the governor made it impossible for the state to serve clients adequately. Her letter of recommendation, which made headlines, declared: "Medicaid is a poor program for poor people."[11]

- During Hurricane Katrina, Douglas Doan, with the Federal Emergency Management Agency (FEMA), fielded an angry call from a Wal-Mart executive about the National Guard "looting" stores in search of baby formula, diapers, and bottled water. Doan challenged the executive to keep the supplies flowing and guaranteed reimbursement. Instead of a commendation, his boss sent investigators to his office threatening legal action. Doan typed out a three line statement: "I did it. . . . I would do it again. The president would agree with it." After several more such incidents, he resigned from federal service.[12]

- In 2003, at the federal Department of Education, career researcher Jon Oberg alerted his superiors that private student loan companies were reaping hundreds of millions of dollars in improper subsidies. He was warned to turn his attention to monitoring research grants. When the overpayments became a public scandal, the department cancelled them by doing what Oberg had recommended four years earlier: send lenders a letter.[13]

These public servants were experts at what they did. All of them took seriously the legal mandates—laws, regulations, and agency protocols—that applied to their work. Yet all five recognized that when the chips are down, it is important to think critically and be able to distinguish your sense of who you are from the role that has been carved out for you by your job. Foucault put it this way, "There is always a little thought even in the most stupid institutions; there is always thought even in silent habits. Criticism is a matter of flushing out that thought and trying to change it: to show that things are not as self-evident as one believed. . . . Practicing criticism is a matter of making facile gestures difficult."[14]

The Ethical Climate

No one can lift from our shoulders the burden of personal responsibility when we work in public service. In that work, which depends heavily on collaborative action within and across organizations, the context of action, or the organizational climate, can be more or less supportive of reflective judgment and choice. For this climate, management must take first responsibility. The chief factor in the organizational context that gets in the way of ethical reflection is the urge to control. Top performance, to use the current buzzword, requires everyone in the agency to get with the program, follow the approved strategy, and adhere to established protocols. That is the message that comes down the chain of command. It is the rare organization, public or private, that genuinely nourishes creative thinking. Hence someone who does so is unusual, particularly when their originality appears to go deeper than the kind of stuff in the suggestion box: a new technical wrinkle that promises to save money or get the job done quicker (the same thing, in the end). The truly original thinker questions *what* is being done, not just *how*. Blocked by official lines of thinking, he or she becomes a guerilla, transgressing policy or administrative mandate.[15]

Organizational orthodoxy turns such a person into an outlier, someone who can be blamed and punished when things go sour—someone like Bunnatine Greenhouse of the Army Corps. We take it for granted that a bureaucrat who dares to speak out, as she did, will be exiled to a do-nothing, powerless job, condemned to sit in an office with desk bare of responsibilities. But despite all the rhetoric about upholding the law and following the regulations, public service also requires reflection and judgment. We must discern the spirit, not just the letter, of the law. An ethical climate in an organization encourages people to think for themselves, consult with others, and support their efforts even when they fail. This sort of recommendation is, of course, unrealistic. It ignores established political-bureaucratic dynamics, which say contract and other administrative decisions are made in favor of major contributors and constituencies and not according to the neutral protocols of bureaucracy. Visible evidence of the pervasiveness of this dynamic is found in a recent Bush administration executive order putting political appointees in charge of reviewing regulations in each federal agency. The order is defended by the Office of Management and Budget as "a classic good-government measure that will make federal agencies more open and accountable." One must ask, To whom and for what?[16]

In response to the charge that an ethical agency climate is unrealistic, my answer is that if this is indeed the case, then why are we wasting time teaching ethics in public administration degree programs? Perhaps our practitioner-students (the vast majority) are patiently spitting back what we teach them, all the while invisibly smirking, perhaps ruefully, at the idea that they could actually be ethical on the job. One academic I know well, who refuses to teach ethics, sums up the plight of the bureaucrat as follows, "I want to be ethical but they won't let me."[17] He is referring to the difficulty of standing up to a command structure that aims for total obedience but saddles the individual with total responsibility. Should we not, in other words, attune ourselves to the reality in public organizations: a complex film of laws, regulations, and protocols, floating haplessly on the surface of a powerful current of politics as usual? If this is the reality, what does meaningful public service consist of?

The answer is not better or more laws, regulations, protocols, and ethical codes. Nor is it training, the typical recourse when organizational leaders discover that their people are not conforming to set standards of whatever kind. In fact there is no answer in the usual sense— no way out, no remedy that will fix the bureaucrat's ethical dilemma.

There might be an approach, however, one that is authentic. It starts with what is given and pretty much unremediable and wrestles with how to live within, and despite, the conditions one has been given. In this respect, working in an agency is no different from life itself. We are all thrown into it, into circumstances we do not choose, and faced with the reality that life, no matter how we live it, is finite. One can try to evade the circumstances, to ignore the inevitable outcome, or one can open oneself to the possibility of building a meaningful life with what is at hand. You take responsibility even though, ultimately, you are not in control. From this perspective laws, rules, and codes are givens with which the individual self is obligated to engage without being determined by them.[18] And the best ethical climate is one that encourages this form of individual responsibility without threatening reprisal.

MEN AND WOMEN IN DARK TIMES

In days made dark by violence, by the doubletalk and camouflage of government leaders, by speech that sweeps important issues under the rug rather than disclosing them in the light of public space, what we have to draw upon is the illumination given us by "men and women, in their lives and in their works."[19] Nowhere is this truer than in public service today, where public servants wrestle with their responsibilities under clouds of antigovernment sentiment, and where obvious darkness, in the form of war, prison camps, torture, the abandonment of citizens to the fury of the storm, and the threat of terrorism, looms over us all.

Arendt offered us stories, believing that there was nothing more powerful with which to counter dark times: Rosa Luxemburg and her passionate engagement in public life, "in the destinies of the world"; Pope John XXIII, with his "strength of daring simplicity," who "never for a moment relinquished his judgment"; Hermann Broch, who wrote that the ultimate ethical principle for human relationships was "helpfulness," the claim to help from one another; Bertolt Brecht, whose plays "crossed the line marking what was permitted to him."[20] In public service we also have stories. Some are in books,[21] but more ready at hand are the many stories in the daily press, of reflective public servants like Greenhouse and Doan thinking for themselves and acting on their best sense of the public good.

In one of Brecht's verses he advises, "Let no one talk you into something, look for yourself; what you don't know yourself you don't know; examine the bill, you'll have to pay for it."[22] These are the words of one who had little if any optimism about the future of humanity but refused to give in to hopelessness. Sardonic he was; cynical, never.

Dewey talked about philosophy as "social hope reduced to a working program of action . . . disciplined by serious thought and knowledge."[23] It seems to me that this is not a bad definition of public service. At least I offer it as a supplement to the idea of public service as the accomplishment of objectives, the efficient use of resources, and the management of the public's business. Public servants continue to be galvanized by social hope, even during the darkest of times, and their work is, at its best, disciplined by serious thought and knowledge, as well as by what Arendt called love of the world.

Our world is not identical with nature. Rather it is a human construct, made up of the web of affairs and interactions among those who inhabit it. "To live together in the world means essentially that a world of things is between those who have it in common, as a table is located between those who sit around it. . . . The public realm, as the common world, gathers us together and yet prevents our falling over each other, so to speak."[24] Action in the public realm is grounded in this world, not only in what others in the world think, but "what the world will be like in the wake of one's acting."[25] The world, the web of relationships we have with others, provides the grounding for public action. It supplies us with intersubjective criteria and a feeling for judging actions or potential actions. Although as we saw in chapter 3 these criteria are not absolute, they do rescue public action from being purely subjective whim. They are the only criteria consistent with maintaining human freedom. Thus, public service must be (as Dewey would have it) "disciplined by serious thought and knowledge" but not determined by the results of scientific studies.

Action reveals the actor. Public words and deeds disclose who somebody is—to others and to the self. In acting, people "show who they are, reveal actively their unique personal identities and thus make their appearance in the human world."[26] Ultimately, then, it seems to me, Arendt's idea of care for the world is connected to what Foucault called "care for the self: . . . an exercise of the self on the self by which one attempts to develop and transform oneself, and to attain to a certain mode of being." Like Arendt and Dewey, Foucault did not see practices of self-development as separate from caring concern for the world. They can be distinguished but not severed from one another, any more than the individual can be separated from the web of human relationships in which he or she is enmeshed. Authentic care for the self equips us to care for the world and to turn practices aimed at personal liberation toward a broader human freedom: "Ethics is the considered form that freedom takes when it is informed by action."[27]

Public service in dark times, then, is mindful, critical, and enacted on common ground—in the world—with others. It is hopeful, serious, and committed to freedom. Foucault would advise us to be modest about our sense of the darkness of these times; he would suggest that "we do not allow ourselves the facile, rather theatrical declaration that this moment in which we exist is one of total perdition, in the abyss of darkness, or a triumphant daybreak, and so on. It is a time like any other, or rather, a time that is never quite like any other."[28] As all the philosophers considered here would agree, it is a time to reflect, to understand the world we live in, and to act responsibly—alone and with others.

Notes

1. Michel Foucault, "Governmentality," in *Michel Foucault: Power*, ed. James D. Faubion (New York: The New Press, 1994).

2. Foucault, "Governmentality," 211.

3. Colin Gordon, "Governmental Rationality: An Introduction," in *The Foucault Effect: Studies in Governmentality*, ed. Graham Burchell, Colin Gordon and Peter Miller (Chicago: University of Chicago Press, 1991), 36.

4. Michel Foucault, "So Is It Important to Think?" in *Michel Foucault: Power*, 455.

5. John Dewey, "The Moral Self," in *The Essential Dewey, Volume II: Ethics, Logic, Psychology*, ed. Larry A. Hickman and Thomas Alexander (Bloomington and Indianapolis, IN: Indiana University Press).

6. Dewey, "The Moral Self," 347.

7. John Dewey, "Moral Judgment and Knowledge," in *The Essential Dewey, Volume II,* 329.

8. James Bernauer and Michael Mahon, "The Ethics of Michel Foucault," in *The Cambridge Companion to Foucault,* ed. Gary Gutting (Cambridge, UK: Cambridge University Press, 1994), 154.

9. Erik Eckholm, "The Conflict in Iraq: The Billions; A Top U.S. Contracting Official for the Army Calls for an Inquiry in the Halliburton Case," *New York Times,* October 25, 2004; Eckholm, "A Watchdog Follows the Money," *New York Times,* November 15, 2004.

10. Sara Keaulani Goo, "Trying to Ground Soaring Costs: The FAA Scrutinizes Contracts after Questions about Unauthorized Charges and Ethics Violations," *Washington Post National Weekly Edition,* August 22–28, 2005, 18–19.

11. Camilla Stivers, "Beverlee Myers: Power, Virtue, and Womanhood in Public Administration," in *Exemplary Public Administrators: Character and Leadership in Government,* ed. Terry L. Cooper and N. Dale Wright (San Francisco: Jossey-Bass, 1992). Rosemary O'Leary, *The Ethics of Dissent* (Washington, DC: CQ Press, 2006) tells several stories of public servants who slowed down, undermined, or put roadblocks in front of measures they believed to be against the public's interest. See also Jennifer Alexander and Samuel Richmond, "Administrative Discretion: Can We Move beyond the Cider House Rules?" *American Review of Public Administration* 37 (2007), 51–64.

12. Christopher Cooper and Robert Block, *Disaster: Hurricane Katrina and the Failure of Homeland Security* (New York: Henry Holt, 2006), 265.

13. Sam Dillon, "Whistle-Blower on Student Aid Is Vindicated," *New York Times,* May 7, 2007, A10.

14. Foucault, "So Is It Important to Think?," 155.

15. O'Leary, *The Ethics of Dissent;* Alexander and Richmond, "Administrative Discretion," note 11.

16. Robert Pear, "Bush Signs Order Increasing Sway at U.S. Agencies," *New York Times,* January 30, 2007, A11.

17. Ralph P. Hummel, "I'd Like to Be Ethical But They Won't Let Me," *International Journal of Public Administration* 12 (1989), 855–66.

18. O. C. McSwite, "The Good, The Bad, and the Neurotic: The Impossibility of Organizational Ethics," typescript from the author.

19. Hannah Arendt, *Men in Dark Times* (San Diego: Harcourt Brace, 1968), ix.

20. Arendt, *Men in Dark Times,* 51, 150, 215.

21. For example, Cooper and Wright, *Exemplary Public Administrators,* note 11; Norma Riccucci, *Unsung Heroes: Federal Execucrats Making a Difference* (Washington, DC: Georgetown University Press, 1995).

22. Arendt, *Men in Dark Times*, 240.

23. Dewey, "Philosophy and Democracy," in *The Essential Dewey, Volume I*, 72–3.

24. Lawrence J. Biskowski, "Practical Foundations for Public Judgment: Arendt on Action and World," *Journal of Politics* 55 (1993), 880.

25. Arendt, *Men in Dark Times*, 236.

26. Hannah Arendt, *The Human Condition* (Chicago: University of Chicago Press, 1958), 179.

27. Michel Foucault, "The Ethics of the Concern for Self as a Practice of Freedom," in *Michel Foucault: Ethics Subjectivity and Truth*, ed. Paul Rabinow (New York: New Press, 1994), 282, 284.

28. Michel Foucault, "Structuralism and Post-structuralism," in *Michel Foucault: Aesthetics, Method, and Epistemology*, ed. James D. Faubion (New York: New Press, 1998), 449.

Index